"A logical plan for daters. Not only will you understand the advice, you will be able to go out and implement what [the authors are] telling you. This is a must-read for all single women."

*David Wygant,*
*the nation's leading dating agent and image-maker*

"The only thing tougher than planning a wedding is living a life with Mr. Wrong. Carol and Jeff will make sure you walk down the aisle with Mr. Right."

*Toni DeLisi,*
*Master Bridal Consultant,*
*President of the NJ Association of Bridal Consultants and*
*Memorable Events, Inc.*

"Ladies, polish up your resumes! *Dating, Inc.* plots out a surefire way to land your dream guy."

*Lisa Daily,*
*dating guru and author of* Stop Getting Dumped!

"Filled with brilliant insights and strategies, *Dating, Inc.* helps us take our hearts temporarily out of the love equation to leave a little room for our heads and offers a modern approach to dating. Jeff [and Carol] Cohen know, when it comes to love, we all can use a business plan."

*Aliza Silverman & Michele Economou,*
*co-hosts,* Single Talk *Radio*

"The business analogy in *Dating, Inc.* is a perfect match for relationship-seeking women currently bonded more to their BlackBerry than to a boyfriend. Whether a woman is just starting out on her search for love or wants to rethink her methods, this husband and wife team gets results."

*Alison Blackman Dunham*
*("Advice Sister Alison" of The Advice Sisters),*
*author,* The Everything® Dating Book, 2nd Edition

"If you are a single woman looking for a loving lifetime partner, read this book. The Cohens give you a road map you can trust to find a partner for life. It worked for them and it can work for you too!"

*Michelle L. Reina, Ph.D.,*
*co-author,* Trust & Betrayal in the Workplace:
Building Effective Relationships in Your Organization, 2nd Edition

"As a head of Recruitment and Selection, I know how important it is to find the right person for the job. Carol and Jeff are the perfect people to show you how to find the right person for a relationship."

*Marietta Cozzi,*
*Vice President,*
*Recruitment and Selection, Fortune 500 company*

"*Dating, Inc.* is practical, funny, and fabulous! If you desire to have both a work life and a love life, then get this book. You deserve to love what you do and be with the one you love."

*Dr. John F. Demartini,*
*bestselling author of*
The Heart of Love–How to Go Beyond Fantasy
to Find True Relationship Fulfillment

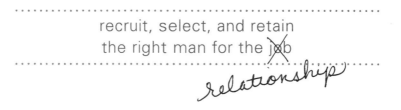

recruit, select, and retain
the right man for the ~~job~~ *relationship*

# dating, inc.

**jeff** cohen
About.com Guide to Dating
& Relationships, and Yahoo!
Personals Columnist

**carol** cohen, M.B.A.

POLKA DOT *press*

Adams Media
Avon, Massachusetts

The Polka Dot Press® name and logo design are registered trademarks
of F+W Publications, Inc.

Published by Polka Dot Press, an imprint of Adams Media,
an F+W Publications Company
57 Littlefield Street
Avon, MA 02322
*www.adamsmedia.com*

ISBN 10: 1-59869-076-0
ISBN 13: 978-1-59869-076-7

Printed in the United States of America.

J   I   H   G   F   E   D   C   B   A

**Library of Congress Cataloging-in-Publication Data**
Cohen, Jeff
Dating, Inc. / Jeff Cohen and Carol Cohen.
p.       cm.
ISBN 1-59869-076-0
1. Dating (Social customs)  I. Cohen, Carol  II. Title.
HQ801.C634 2006
646.7'7082—dc22
2006014735

This publication is designed to provide accurate and authoritative
information with regard to the subject matter covered. It is sold with
the understanding that the publisher is not engaged in rendering legal,
accounting, or other professional advice. If legal advice or other expert
assistance is required, the services of a competent professional person
should be sought.

> —From a *Declaration of Principles* jointly adopted
> by a Committee of the American Bar Association
> and a Committee of Publishers and Associations

Many of the designations used by manufacturers and sellers to distinguish their product are claimed as trademarks. Where those designations appear in this book and Adams Media was aware of a trademark
claim, the designations have been printed with initial capital letters.

*This book is available at quantity discounts for bulk purchases.*
*For information, please call 1-800-289-0963.*

# dedication

This book is dedicated to all the smart, savvy businesswomen who will no longer have to depend on fate to find a mate. Stay strong and motivated! We know he's out there somewhere.

This book is also dedicated with love to Miriam, Victor, Janis, and Bert, the smart, savvy parents who raised us, as well as Diana and Alyssa, our super-savvy sisters.

# contents

# for your information (fyi)

This book is just the start of your journey toward finding a great guy. Check out these other good resources to help you along the way:

- Visit *www.datingincbook.com* for more tips on applying business principles to dating and relationships, additional products and services, an information-packed newsletter, dating and relationship seminars in your area, and dating coaching.
- Visit *www.boldroad.com,* Jeff's writing, speaking, and consulting company, which helps people reach their career, love, and life potential. Bold Road uses straightforward, no-nonsense business principles to help individual and corporate clients achieve bold results.
- Visit *www.dating.about.com* for the latest dating and relationship articles from Jeff Cohen, About.com's Guide to Dating and Relationships. You'll see original content on everything from meeting someone new and online dating to getting serious and engagement.
- Visit *www.fastinternetdating.com* to get seven free special reports on internet dating secrets, including everything from writing a killer profile to unlocking the date of your dreams.

# acknowledgments

In the business world, acknowledgments translate best as Reward and Recognition. This is the time when companies and small businesses take a step back from profit making to distinguish those most responsible for the company's success. The 5 to 10 percent of employees who are recognized feel truly appreciated for their efforts. Unfortunately, the 90 to 95 percent of employees who get left out can sometimes feel underappreciated.

But let's be honest. Academy Award winners forget to acknowledge their husbands all the time when they're up there at the podium, so surely you can forgive us when we overlook one or two people, too. To the people we're about to leave out, we hope you still know in your hearts that we appreciate and love you.

Without further ado, here are the individuals most responsible for our success and that of this book.

First, thank you to our grandparents and great-grandparents, who are no longer with us. If not for the dating choices made by Hannah, Mendel, Ben, Nesriya, Baba, Fred, and Benjamin, our parents and their offspring (that's right—the authors) would not exist.

Thank you to Alice "Gram-Gram" Winitt who wrote a heartfelt, foreshadowing letter to her grandson in 1982 saying, "Jeff, you should be a writer." We thank you for the advice and apologize for taking twenty-five years to make it happen.

Thank you to our parents, Miriam, Victor, Janis, and Bert. Collectively, you taught us to take chances, install new locks, follow our dreams, cook delicious vegetable soup, live responsibly, understand sports, show patience, remodel an unfinished basement, and put family first. Thanks also to Daniel for loving Miriam and Jacqueline for loving Victor.

Thank you to our sisters, Diana and Alyssa. Diana is the most creative person we know and has the ability to brighten an entire room with her presence. We love getting our mail because you're always sending us inspiring, artistic letters and cards. Alyssa is our pace car, having traveled the path of marriage and parenthood to show us the way. Thanks also to Jeff for popping the question to Alyssa and helping produce our first nieces, Samantha and Rebecca. Please don't give them a copy of this book until 2021, when they're old enough to date!

Thank you to all of our extended family around the globe, including our many cousins, aunts, and uncles. Your love and support means the world to us.

Thank you to Fluffy, Nikki, Lucky, Jasmine, and Meatball, our childhood pets, for teaching us unconditional love and how to share a bed. Long before we spooned with each other, we cuddled with you.

Thank you to Marietta Cozzi, our beloved Cupid. She's not only a vice president of recruitment and selection at work, but she recruited and selected us for each other. We are forever grateful for the introduction. If not for you, we might have worked two floors apart at American Express for years without ever crossing paths. Thanks also to Deb Foley, who secured a second date for us by exchanging our phone numbers.

Thank you to all of the smart, savvy businesswomen, businessmen, friends, and family who so honestly shared their business wisdom and dating war stories. Together, you make up our SuperStar Network, the people we can rely on for great advice and loyal encouragement. The richness of your submissions and willingness to share the good and bad of your experiences helped the book's concepts leap right off the page and into the minds of the reader. (Plus, without your honesty and insights, our book would be a hundred pages shorter.)

By the way, just to protect that wonderful honesty, we changed all of your names throughout the book. Still, we wanted to put your names in print to thank you for so generously offering your help. So thank you all across the globe to Jason Amici, Gil Beverly, Vicky Biggs, Cris Canals, Alexina and Su Chai, Marietta Cozzi, Deb Foley, Aimee and Greg Gatti, John Guilfoy, Alyssa Horvath, Katherine Kim, Chelsea and Marc Klatzko, Jan Klein, Debi Lee, Diana Mimon, Shruti Patel, Brad Prutkin, Christy and Jeff Rosen, Gunce and Mark Rosen, Jen and Scott Ross, Mike Weinbach, and Mary Wilson. If anyone can successfully match all of these names to their stories in the book, we'll send you a free, autographed copy of *Dating, Inc.* We'd also like to recommend you find a few new hobbies.

Thank you to our extended SuperStar Network, people who supported and contributed to our journey as authors, colleagues, speakers, and consultants. Thanks also to those of you on the list who regularly checked in on our progress as we embarked on writing this book. If you're reading this now and see your name, there's no need to ask any more. We finished it! In alphabetical order, some of the people we'd like to specifically thank are Jackie Altschul, Kelly Arnone, Tony and Kim Avilez, Patty Bales, Aaron Brown, Mary Bryant, Dr. Frank Candido, Toni DeLisi, Sherry Derby, Rad Dewey, Zuleika Fertullien, Shai Fischer, Ian Flaherty, Lewis Harrison, Helen and John Harvey, John Havens, Jennifer Henslee, Page Hite, Deidre and George Hykal, Jose Irizarry, Aisha Bastiaans and Kevin Jacobson, Amber Jennings, Ilan Judkiewicz, Peter Klaus, Graham Klein, Debi Lee, Dr. Scott Lippe, Marc Madison, Sharon Naylor, Katharine "PH" Nisbet, Robin Parness, Dennis Paul, Deirdre Reilly, Dennis and Michelle Reina, Kris Root, Pamela Rosenau, Rona Rubin, Vansiny Saukam, Herve Sedky, Judith and Jim, Shelly Stanton, Harriet Stark, Bill Tompkins, John Webster, Roger Weems, and Erik Zerrenner.

Thank you to the late Marian Karpen for giving us a forum to spread our message about getting on the Bold Road of life. Thanks also to the late Kim Vismale and her husband Danny Vismale for inspiring us to define our legacy.

Thank you to the wonderful bosses and mentors at American Express who touched our lives and positively impacted our personal development, including Michael Barry, Ellen Bloom, Jim Dwyer, Maggie Gagliardi, Gaby Giglio, Ash Gupta, Tom Leitko, Kim Lewis, Victoria Linssen, Steve Power, Christine Robinson, Colleen Rumbal, Susan Sobbott, and Richard Williams. We are proud to admit that we actually liked our bosses at work!

Thank you to Sue Kim for telling us about the Dating and Relationships Expert opening at About.com. Landing that gig was one of the first big steps in getting our message out there. You also make a delicious Dok Boki, which re-energized our spirits and stomachs on those days when writer's block appeared. Thanks also to the About.com team, especially Michael Daecher, Marc Goldberg, Matt Law, Avram Piltch, Gina Carey, and Caryn Solly. You are truly a SuperStar team, and we're proud to be working with you.

Thank you to Mark Levy, who inspires innovation and creativity in everyone he meets. You made us better writers and invited us to Book Expo, where we met Adams Media. That makes you a great man and an even better middleman.

Thank you to a great team at Adams Media. All of you have championed this book from the very beginning. Your enthusiasm is contagious, and we thank you for believing in us. To Gary Krebs, Kirsten Amann, and Brielle Kay, you are truly a dynamic trio. From pitching the concept to your publishing board to countless valuable edits, you have been tremendous partners throughout this journey. We hope you enjoyed the ride with us as much as we did with you. Thanks also to the wonderful sales and marketing team at Adams, led by Scott Watrous, including Beth Gissinger, Karen Cooper, Jeanne Emmanuel, Steve Quinn, Michael Kelly, Stephanie McKenna, and Kim Sorrell. You really helped spread the word about *Dating, Inc.* and we are truly grateful for your efforts.

Thank you to our expert legal and accounting team for your wisdom and guidance. Thanks to Helen Wan for your keen contractual insights and Larry Ginsburg for keeping business expenses separate from personal expenses. Remind us to give you some receipts the next time we see you.

Thank you to Catalyst, an organization that "seeks a world that supports and encourages every woman in her career aspirations and places no limits on where her skills and energy can take her." We are grateful for the use of your insightful research in our sidebars and for encouraging women everywhere to reach their potential.

Finally, thanks to you, the reader, for opening your heart and mind to the thoughts in this book. You are well on the way to taking charge of your love life. (Although if you're reading this at the office right now, you should put the book down and get back to work.) On second thought, hold the book up high for your fellow business colleagues to see. Maybe we can start a cubicle-to-cubicle ad campaign—it could be the word-of-mouth approach of the new millennium! Better yet, get a copy of this book for all your single girlfriends. You can take charge of your love lives together. Pretty soon you'll be a force to be reckoned with on the singles scene!

# introduction—
# opening remarks

From: your.boss@work.com
To: you@work.com
Subject: New Marketing Analyst
i got 30 secs b4 a meeting. i want u to find a new
marketing analyst. can u put tgthr some ideas by
5 o'clok and leeve em on my desk.
Tanks for making it happen.

Imagine receiving this e-mail. Ignore the fact that it's full of spelling mistakes, cryptic abbreviations, and has an inexplicable allergy to capitalization. Anyone with a boss knows that ambiguous e-mails fired haphazardly from their BlackBerries are their preferred method of communication.

If you've ever hired an employee or held a job, I'll bet you could satisfy this request for a marketing analyst and crank out a full-fledged action plan. You would hand your boss a neat little folder outlining the job description, qualifications, recruitment channels, and interview schedule.

Now imagine receiving this e-mail from your boss:

From: your.boss@work.com
To: you@work.com
Subject: Getting Married
i got 30 secs b4 a meeting. i want u to find a spouse.
can u put tgthr some ideas by 5 o'clok and leeve em
on my desk.
Tanks for making it happen.

Will your boss still get that neat little folder with an action plan by five o'clock? Or is your mind now swirling with the magnitude of this request? Keep in mind that only a few words in the e-mail have changed. However, I'll bet your reaction to each e-mail is completely different. Why is that?

## Don't Mind Your Swirling Mind

To find the answer, let's meet Melissa, Jessica, and Sandra.

### Who Is Melissa?

At work, Melissa is a dynamo. She's a vice president at a global financial services firm, leads high-performing project teams, and knows how to get the job done. Melissa is well regarded by her leaders and admired by her staff. Her boss is even eyeing her for a promotion.

At home, though, Melissa is a completely different person. Her typical Friday night is spent solo and entails a bottle of wine, reruns of *Sex and the City,* and a pint of chocolate-chip ice cream. On the rare occasion Melissa does go on a date, it doesn't lead to anything.

### Who Is Jessica?

Jessica is a savvy small-business owner in London. Five years ago she left her steady job to open a trendy retail shop in Covent Garden. Riding the success of her first store, she recently opened a second shop. Her customers and suppliers admire her optimism, dedication, and ambition.

On the dating scene, Jessica meets lots of potential husbands and even came close to walking down the aisle once. Since breaking off her engagement, Jessica has poured her energy into the stores. She readily tells her friends that Mr. Right will someday come into one of her stores. Their eyes will meet, and they'll just know.

### Who Is Sandra?

Sandra works at a mid-sized advertising firm outside Chicago. She's creative, dependable, and knows how to drive results. Sandra loves her job but doesn't feel the need to someday run the firm. As long as her projects are interesting, she's content to work successfully at her current level.

Six years ago, at the age of twenty-eight, Sandra and her husband divorced. Sandra's mother, also divorced, is currently battling breast cancer and has temporarily moved in with her daughter. Between chemotherapy appointments with her mom and forty to fifty hours per week at work, little time is left for dating.

## What Do Melissa, Jessica, and Sandra Have in Common?

Melissa, Jessica, and Sandra are all successful at work. They know how to set goals and achieve them, focus on customer service, and use solid business skills to get the job done. What they don't realize is that they can use the same skills that help them flourish at work to land the man of their dreams. By tackling an emotional topic like love with a logical, business-minded approach, their results in love can match their achievements in the office.

Whenever I talk about logic versus emotion, people say to me, "Hey Jeff, love is still a matter of the heart. You can't treat love like a business transaction." Let me be the first to say that I completely agree! Love is a matter of the heart. The person you choose to date seriously or eventually marry should of course be decided emotionally. However, this book is all about approaching the dating scene from a logical place. I'm going to show you how to logically apply business principles you already know or can easily learn to meet more great guys and find the right one for you. Then, once you find the right guy, you can by all means let the emotions (and the sparks) fly. That kinetic connection is what will keep the relationship strong for years to come.

### Are You Just Like Melissa, Jessica, or Sandra?

When you read Melissa, Jessica, and Sandra's stories, I'll bet one of three thoughts immediately crossed your mind:

1. I am Melissa (or Jessica, or Sandra).
2. My story is different from Melissa's, Jessica's, and Sandra's, but I can relate to how they feel.
3. Did I save my receipt for this book?

If you chose thought one or two, you are definitely reading the right book. If you chose thought three, let me be the first to tell you that all sales are final—and this is your future we are talking about. In case you're still not convinced, here's a quick true-false test to see if *Dating, Inc.* is the right book for you. For each question, circle either "true" or "false":

1. I feel good about my career path, but not my romance results.
   **TRUE**      **FALSE**
2. I'm not happy with either my career path or my romance results.
   **TRUE**      **FALSE**
3. People always tell me I deserve a great guy, but I haven't found him yet.
   **TRUE**      **FALSE**
4. I'm with the wrong guy and know I need to get out of this relationship.
   **TRUE**      **FALSE**
5. I'm divorced, widowed, or recently broke up with someone and feel ready to start dating again.
   **TRUE**      **FALSE**

If you circled "true" for at least one of the five questions, then this book is for you. If you circled "false" for at least one of the five questions, then this book is also for you. Why? You just wrote in the book, now you really can't return it. Gotcha!

## Now That I'm Officially Keeping This Book, What Is It About?

*Dating, Inc.* is written for Melissa, Jessica, Sandra, you, and the millions of other single women across the globe. You are desirable, likeable, and successful in your jobs, but for some reason, when it comes to love, there is a disconnect. Whether it's because you're settling for the wrong guy, latching on to just an okay guy, or avoiding the dating scene entirely, you aren't getting what you deserve in your relationships.

Let's get one thing straight right away. This book is not just for currently super-successful single businesswomen! If you have ever held a job, any job at all at any point in your career, you'll relate to the concepts in this book. More simply, if you've ever held a job, then you can find a man. From corporate vice presidents to restaurant waitresses, we're all familiar with customers, sales, hiring and firing, and bosses. This book will show you how the concepts you've already mastered in your everyday life will help you recruit, select, and retain the right man for a relationship. Also, don't think you have to fall under "never been married" to benefit from this book. If you're single, separated, divorced, or widowed, keep reading! As long as you're looking for that special someone, this book is for you.

Regardless of your dating past, *Dating, Inc.* will teach you how to apply the business skills you already know, or could easily learn, to land more dates and ultimately find your soul mate. You already know how to create success in your lives; you've done it in your career, with friends, and among family. I'm going to teach you how to redirect those same success skills to your love life. Think of it as Strategic Dating!

## Can Business Principles Really Lead to Dating Success?

How do I know that business principles can lead to dating success? I'm proof positive because I've used such principles myself. Let me explain. A few years ago, I was in a successful career, climbing the corporate ladder. I had recently graduated from Wharton Business School and was a director at a financial services company in New York City. I became an expert in project management and driving results. No matter the request, initiative, project, or task, I could visualize the desired end goal, break it down into action steps, and execute on the plan to make it happen.

Despite my success at work, something was missing in my personal life. I really wanted to get married and start a family. Unfortunately, I didn't even have a girlfriend at the time. After many emotional days and months complaining to my friends and family, it hit me: *I'm using all these business principles successfully at work. Why not apply them to finding the woman of my dreams?* That was the precise moment I visualized that e-mail from my boss asking me to find a spouse. For the first time, I thought about dating in business terms. Light bulbs were flashing in my head telling me I was on to something big. Suddenly, my entire outlook on dating and single life was changed forever.

Don't get me wrong—I did not view my search for a wife as a business transaction. Just like Jerry Maguire, I wanted someone to "complete me." I also knew that it wasn't going to be Renée Zellweger and that complaining to my friends and depending on fate was getting me no closer to finding her.

### Jeff's Dating Plan Comes to Life

Using tactics I learned in my business education and during my on-the-job corporate experience, I designed a methodical dating program to attract more women and find the one of my dreams. Complete with goals and objectives, an action plan, and timeline, my dating program consisted of actions such as these:

- 3 trips to singles-themed Club Med resorts
- 1 gold membership in a dating service
- 4 Hamptons summer shares and one New Jersey Shore house
- 300 nights in Manhattan and New Jersey pubs ogling, flirting, and in some cases leaving with phone numbers scribbled on napkins and coasters
- 77 blind dates

The dating program paid off for me. Blind date number seventy-eight turned out to be Carol, who later became my wife (and now my coauthor).

### Meet #78

I know exactly what you're thinking: "It's great that this dating program panned out for you, Jeff, but you're a guy, and dating is totally different for men." Touché. Luckily, I anticipated this potential question, and hired (I mean married) a secret weapon, Carol Cohen. Throughout *Dating, Inc.* Carol offers the female perspective, told in her own words, through Carol's "Corporate Memo." Carol's voice is integral to the messages in this book for four main reasons:

1. *Dating, Inc.* is written for the savvy, successful business-woman. I can strive to be savvy, work toward success, and run a business, but that woman thing is a bit of a stretch.
2. Carol already gets half the profits from *Dating, Inc.*, so she really should have to write at least some of the 60,000 words.
3. Carol used to be just like Melissa, Jessica, and Sandra. She was a high-flying business consultant, flourishing at work, but longing to find her life partner. She did rack up thousands of frequent-flier miles (which I'm happy to benefit from now), but she also realized her long-term happiness depended on more than just first-class upgrades.
4. Carol has an M.B.A. and really knows her stuff when it comes to business concepts. Do I have an M.B.A. too? The answer is no, but I did marry one, and that should count for something.

While I can be the voice of the dating expert, and living proof that a business-style dating plan really works, Carol will represent the women. She's living proof that a successful businesswoman can translate her corporate success into relationships, too. Without further ado, here's Carol's first memo.

## Corporate Memo

TO: All Employees
FROM: Carol Cohen
RE: Your Love Life

I used to think it was easier to rely on fate than to attempt a dating plan. After all, if it's meant to be, won't your Prince Charming simply appear? Isn't that what we've been taught since we were innocent little girls reading stories like Sleeping Beauty, where Prince Charming really does just magically appear?

I was a strategic business consultant, flying all over the place on projects helping companies create and execute strategies to improve their business. At the time, I was so focused on my career that I barely spent a minute trying to meet someone. As if that were not enough to keep me single, I had all these silly dating rules that kept me out of the game. Next thing I know, two years go by without even a single date. Yes, I'm climbing the ladder at work, but I'm not getting any closer to finding a man. When I did try to date, I did everything wrong. I played games. I acted too busy for guys. I'm not proud of this, but I even convinced myself on many occasions that I was too busy to date!

Basically, I had no dating plan, and my results demonstrated my lack of an approach. This lack of an approach, while hopelessly romantic, was completely incongruous with everything that has made me a successful businessperson! Here I was, able to help other companies with their business success, but working entirely without a strategy for my own dating success.

While it can feel overwhelming to tackle finding a soul mate, it can also be incredibly empowering if you keep in mind the business skills that already make you a success at work. Women like us have this amazing ability to be proactive on the job and get things done. There's absolutely no reason we can't apply those same skills to romance. After all, I can't imagine a more important client, customer, or project than you!

My column is dedicated to YOU! I hope to motivate and encourage you, share tender and courageous stories, provide hopeful insights, and energize you on the successful and exhilarating journey that lies ahead of you, starting today.

---

### What a Woman!

Okay, I might be biased, but I just love that woman. Did I mention that Carol and I are 9-11 survivors? I'm not going to relive the whole experience, but let's just say we were in the Twin Towers at the time the first plane hit. We reversed the numbers and got married on 11-9 to honor our fallen colleagues. From that horrific day on September 11, 2001, we vowed to celebrate life, enjoy the ride, and share our message.

### The International Language of Business

Okay, you've met me, and you've met Carol. You're also still reading this book and that's a great sign of your commitment to try a new approach. At this point, it's my job to hook you on the Dating Business Plan that's about to be unveiled.

I could just lay it out in bullet points, or a list, but I want to speak the international language of business. We all know that's PowerPoint. So here's our PowerPoint presentation on what you can expect in this book.

**Dating, Inc. Business Plan**

Prepared by:

Jeff Cohen and Carol Cohen

### Dating, Inc. Agenda

*Dating, Inc.* is organized into three main sections:

- The Self-Assessment: Taking stock of yourself
- The Action Plan: Getting out there and executing the plan
- The One: Having a great relationship when you find a great guy

Each section includes three chapters. In each chapter we'll describe a common business term, explain the related dating term, and then show you how to implement the terms in your personalized dating approach.

## Section 1: The Self-Assessment

The Self-Assessment section includes three chapters:

|     | Business Principle | Dating Principle |
| --- | --- | --- |
| #1 | Mission Statement | Wishin' Statement |
| #2 | Goals and Objectives | Souls and Objectives |
| #3 | Research and Development | Research and Envelopment |

## Section 2: The Action Plan

The Action Plan section includes three chapters:

|     | Business Principle | Dating Principle |
| --- | --- | --- |
| #4 | Market Plan | Spark-It Plan |
| #5 | Recruitment and Selection | Recruitment and Affection |
| #6 | Management | Manage-Men |

## Section 3: The One

Our The One section includes three chapters:

|  | Business Principle | Dating Principle |
|---|---|---|
| #7 | Customer Service | Lust-omer Service |
| #8 | Talent Assessment | Talent Assess-Men |
| #9 | Joint Venture | Joint Adventure |

## Appendix 1

At the end of *Dating, Inc.* you'll see a blank Dating Business Plan. This is your chance to take action on what you've learned and design your personalized dating business plan, including:

| Wishin' Statement | Spark-It Plan | Lust-omer Service |
|---|---|---|
| Souls & Objectives | Recruitment & Affection | Talent Assess-Men |
| Research & Envelopment | Manage-Men | Joint Adventure |

### How to Use This Book

Hopefully the PowerPoint presentation gave you a sense of what you can expect from *Dating, Inc.* As an added bonus—and at no additional charge if you act now—we've thrown in three additional appendices. So if the book and Dating Business Plan aren't enough to satisfy your dating desires, check out the back of the book for these exciting extras:

- **Business Terms Applied to Dating:** A quick hit list of our favorite business terms and their application to the world of dating and relationships.
- **Start Your Own SuperStar Network Book Club:** How to start your own SuperStar Network Book Club and what to talk about together at your first meeting. What's that, you don't know what book to read together first? How about *Dating, Inc?*
- **An Interview with Carol and Jeff Cohen:** Get to know your authors better, with answers to the most common questions we're asked by our readers and the media.

### Extra Resources

Every project or plan can benefit from extra resources to get the job done. This book is no exception, so we've included some unique tools to bring the business and dating concepts to life. Think of these extra resources as helping hands, just like when you add an extra employee to a project team to help get the job done. Throughout the book, you can expect to find the following additional resources.

### Corporate Memos

You've already been introduced to "Corporate Memo" earlier in this chapter. As you can see, Carol is completely focused on your success as you take charge of your love life. Throughout the book, she will use her column to share dating case studies and woman-to-woman advice.

### Work/Life Balance

We all need to strike a balance between working hard and finding quality time away from the office. So in every chapter, before we jump into the business and dating terms, we'll open with a word jumble. Your job will be to unscramble the letters in the jumble. In doing so, you'll discover the main theme or message for the chapter you're about to read while also having some fun along the way.

Here's a quick word jumble for practice. Unscramble the three words and write your answer in the blank space provided:

N Y O J E   E T H   D R E I _____

What did you come up with? In the conclusion of this book, you'll find the answer key for the Work/Life Balance word jumbles. Once you've solved this jumble, you'll know the motto that Carol and I live by in everything we do. We also hope it's a motto you'll follow as you undertake the opportunities laid out in *Dating, Inc.*

### Check Your Inbox

We opened *Dating, Inc.* with two illustrative e-mails from your boss, one with a business request, the other with a dating request. This model will continue throughout the book. In each chapter, we'll open with a typical business e-mail request you might receive from your boss. We'll then translate that business request into a dating-related e-mail to fully illustrate how the business principle translates to dating and relationships.

### Jeff's Defs

What's a Wishin' Statement? How is recruitment and selection different from Recruitment and Affection? What does it mean to go on a Joint Adventure? In business and in dating, there are terms you need to know, and Jeff's Defs will be your source for definitions. Think of it as a glossary traveling with you throughout the book.

### Agenda/ The Bottom Line

In business, you might be familiar with the terms agenda and the bottom line. The agenda is your starting point, your current state. The bottom line is where you hope to be at the end of your journey. Each chapter will open with an agenda to set up the starting point and will close with a bottom line to make sure you've arrived at the right place to move on to the next chapter.

### Let's Talk Offline

Have you ever been in a meeting where two people get into a conversation that's off topic? Then one of the people says, "Let's continue this conversation offline." We'll do the same thing in *Dating, Inc.* This will be our chance to share additional stories, statistics, and information that further illustrate the concepts in the book.

### Action Item

I'd love to tell you that everything we say in this book qualifies as a bright idea. However, there will be some points we make that are the real juicy ones, the creative ideas you don't want to miss. We'll mark these innovative thoughts as Action Items. This will serve as your motivational wakeup call to focus in on the information about to be shared.

### Women's Intuition

As you know, throughout the book, Carol will share her perspective through "Corporate Memo." While I personally believe Carol has what it takes to represent the voice of super-successful, savvy businesswomen, we decided to get a few more perspectives. So we relied on a business principle, networking, to gather feedback and valuable insights from single and married women all across the globe. We will share many of their stories, advice, and anecdotes throughout to further bring the book's concepts to life.

We should also say that we had some guys chime in to offer their perspectives. Why? Well, there's nothing wrong with hearing the guy's side of the story here and there. Plus, we have all these male friends who couldn't keep their mouths shut.

The men who chimed in, plus the females of Women's Intuition together make up our SuperStar Network, the kind and generous people we thanked in the acknowledgments. Our SuperStar Network is our support system. They're people we grew up with, went to summer camp with, went to college with, worked with, met on a plane, bumped into on a vacation, or simply reached out to in an effort to expand our network of great contacts. We firmly believe everyone should have his or her own SuperStar Network. We can't make it through life alone. The more people we know, the more people we can all learn from and rely on.

### *State of the Business*

In each chapter we'll highlight one major demographic statistic and apply it directly to the chapter. This is your chance to see the macro-impact of the concepts we're sharing.

## Are You Ready to Take Charge of Your Love Life? We Can't Hear You!

So there you have it, a full breakdown of what you can expect from *Dating, Inc.* We'll give you all the tools you need, but one major question remains. Are you ready to take charge of your love life and try a new approach to dating and relationships? I can't hear you. I said, are you ready to take charge of your love life and make some changes?

If you just screamed out "Yes!!" then please apologize to the kind woman next to you on the train, your roommate, or the cute guy in the next aisle at the bookstore.

Since I'm fairly certain I won't hear you yelling, I've devised a simple test to see if you're really ready to take some action. Here are two pie charts. One is filled in as an illustration, the other is for you to complete.

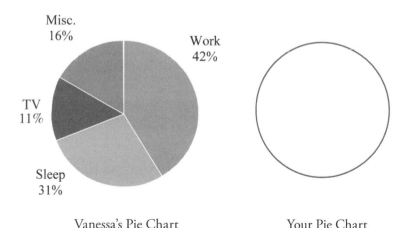

Vanessa's Pie Chart                     Your Pie Chart

We've all seen pie charts used in business to analyze everything from real estate trends to company financials to the ups and downs of the stock market. In *Dating, Inc.,* we're examining a pie chart of how a single woman might spend her typical day. The illustration shows you the actual pie chart for a single businesswoman named Vanessa. She's a director at a mid-sized real estate agency in Washington, D.C. Now in her late thirties, Vanessa spent the last fifteen years going after the million-dollar sales club at her agency. A decade and a half later, she has the hard-earned plaque on her mantel but nobody to share it with. You can see in the illustration how Vanessa spends the typical twenty-four hours in a day: predominantly working and sleeping, with some TV and miscellaneous activities mixed in. When I asked Vanessa about her pie chart, she said, "I've been so busy with work in the last fifteen years, there just hasn't been time to date! Don't get me wrong, I made a choice to pursue my career in real estate to the best of my ability, and am 100 percent satisfied with my success. However, when I think about what I really want out of my life, and think about how I've been spending my time, I'm not sure it's been spent in a way that will ultimately make me happy." Now it's your turn. Start dividing up the blank pie chart based on how you spend your typical day.

If your pie chart looks anything like Vanessa's, it's missing one major slice of pie. If you're not devoting any part of your day to actively seeking your ideal guy, then you have significantly diminished your chances of finding him. If you don't put in the time, why would you expect to see any results? Let that truly sink in, because it's one of the most important points in this entire book.

Think about the difference between the high performers at work and the average employees. The high performers always seem to drive the most results, show the most positive energy, work the extra hours, and have an overall reputation for making things happen. In short, high performers take action. That's what separates them from the average employee, the people just skating by or coasting at work.

Look, I know you're a smart, savvy woman who knows from the business environment that a lack of action equals a lack of results. I promise you that if you're willing to take that business mindset and apply it right now, the results will be extraordinary. So commit right now that you'll give this Dating Business Plan the same effort you put forth at work. You, and the great guy you meet, will be very thankful. I can't wait for you to e-mail me at *contact@datingincbook.com* with your dating success story.

## The Opportunity Cost

If you've ever taken an economics class, then you're probably familiar with the term opportunity cost. In simplest terms, opportunity cost represents the benefit that could be derived from choosing to do something else besides reading this book and taking charge of your love life. In other words, you're about to devote a certain number of hours (or days, depending on your reading speed) to reading *Dating, Inc.* I want to tell you exactly why that time commitment is absolutely worth it!

Here are the ten opportunities that lie ahead for you after reading this book:

1. You will land more dates.
2. You will attract better-quality partners.
3. You will find the courage to end a bad relationship and move on to the right guy for you.
4. You'll dramatically increase your odds of finding your soul mate.
5. You will get to know your dating style better and improve your chances of meeting the ideal type for your preferences.
6. You will read a book instead of flipping on the TV.
7. You'll learn a few new vocabulary words.
8. You will have exciting dating stories, advice, and success tips to offer when somebody asks, "How can I take charge of my love life too?"
9. Uh oh, I need another idea for this list, help me out Carol!
10. How about the most important one you almost forgot to share, "Your success in dating will match your achievements in the office!" Phew! Thanks, Carol, for jumping in there.

Okay, I'll admit the first five reasons (plus Carol's reason at the end) are much more important than reasons six through nine. But don't you think that the first five opportunities are enough to read this book? What would it really be worth to you if you could land more dates, attract better-quality partners, end a bad relationship, find your soul mate, and maybe even learn about yourself and your dating preferences?

## Let's Get It Started

It's time for us to open for business. So let's get started on the first business concept in *Dating, Inc.*: the mission statement. Without a vision of your desired guy, how do you know why you're dating in the first place?

In Chapter 1, you'll learn how companies develop their mission statements and how you can enter the dating scene with a Wishin' Statement.

# The Self-Assessment

## Welcome to Section 1, the Self-Assessment

The self-assessment is all about understanding you and what you want in a partner. Before we can jump into action, and I know a high performer like you is ready to act, we need to take a step back. We need to review your dating past, figure out your dating strengths, and determine the kind of partner who is right for you. Companies don't just jump into action without a plan, and neither should you. Have no fear; you're not about to endure full-fledged psychoanalysis here. (Although if you do want that, we happen to know a great therapist looking for new patients.)

Section 1, the Self-Assessment, includes three main business and dating principles we'll cover together:

1. Biz Principle #1—Mission Statement
   Dating Principle #1—Wishin' Statement
2. Biz Principle #2—Goals and Objectives
   Dating Principle #2—Souls and Objectives
3. Biz Principle #3—Research and Development
   Dating Principle #3—Research and Envelopment

By the end of this section, you'll know exactly the guy you're looking for, what it will take to find him, the dating strengths you have to offer, and some opportunities to improve your chances on the dating scene. How's that for a sales promise?

## Corporate Memo

TO: All Employees

FROM: Carol Cohen

RE: Your Love Life

We put lots of thought into our career path as women. Whether it's moving up in our organization, starting a new business, or simply finding a job we love, we know how to set our sights on a goal and go after it. It's exactly that type of thinking that has helped all of us in breaking through the glass ceiling and led to even more women in senior roles and prominent positions in the workplace.

There is absolutely no reason we can't put the same thought into what we want and deserve in our relationships. That's what these first three chapters are really all about. Instead of completely avoiding the dating scene because you've been burned or just dating anyone and hoping for the best, you're going to visualize the guy you want, figure out what it will take to land that guy, and then put yourself in the best possible position to convert great dates with a quality guy into a meaningful relationship.

So let's take that same go-getter attitude at work and apply it fearlessly and directly to dating!

# chapter
# **one**

Biz Principle #1:
**mission statement**

Dating Principle #1:
**wishin' statement**

## Agenda

- Defining the purpose of a company mission statement
- Completing a self-assessment to identify your dating starting point
- Developing your own dating code of conduct
- Determining the role your dating Wishin' Statement plays in landing a great guy
- Providing tools to get started in crafting your own Wishin' Statement

## Work/Life Balance

Let's pretend it's 9:04 on Monday morning, and you just arrived at the office. The red light is already blinking on your voicemail, a blatant reminder that your weekend is now a distant memory. You log on to check your e-mail. Fifty-seven unread messages appear, twenty-one of which are marked urgent. Meanwhile, your boss just slipped you a sticky note that says, "Drop by when you have a chance. I've got an ad-hoc assignment for you." You're four minutes into your week and already way behind.

Rather than listen to your voicemail, respond to e-mails, or pop into your boss' office, you decide to ease into your week. You're still a SuperStar at work, but nobody gets your time before you finish your coffee. While sipping on a mocha latte you complete the word jumble from today's paper. By 9:10 A.M. you'll be a high performer again, but right now there's nothing wrong with a little work-life balance.

The same theory holds in *Dating, Inc.* You're about to strategically apply business principles to your dating approach. Still, there's nothing wrong with taking some time for yourself and enjoying a little creative diversion. So before we jump into learning about company mission statements and dating Wishin' Statements, here's your word jumble to get you motivated and help you ease into the chapter:

TSOHO RFO HTE RTSSA  _____

If you're having trouble with this word jumble, remember the answer key is located in the back of this book—unlike the newspaper, which makes you buy the next edition to get the answers. Without giving anything away, let's just say this word jumble represents an important approach to writing a company mission statement or dating Wishin' Statement. You want to think big because you deserve it. If you don't set your expectations high now, then you're really just settling. Nobody deserves that fate when it comes to dating!

## The Importance of a Company Mission Statement

From: your.boss@work.com
To: you@work.com
Subject: New Project Mission
I'm off 2 a meting. Giv sum thought 2 our kompany mishin.
Tanks for making it happen.

Once again, you've got a vague e-mail from your boss. At least the e-mails are consistent in that the spelling mistakes and capitalization allergy are present. One thing we do know from this memo is that the boss is looking for your help in updating the company mission. So, how might you approach this assignment in the workplace? Just to make sure we're all on the same page here, let's start with the definition of a company mission statement.

> **JEFF'S DEF•I•NI•TIONS:** According to the Society for Human Resource Management, a company mission or vision statement refers to what an organization wants to become or hopes to accomplish in the future.

As you can tell from the definition, a company mission statement is an aspiration. It truly represents why the company is in business in the first place. Let's take a look at the mission statements for some well-known, successful companies (taken from their Web sites and annual reports):

- **Google:** Google's mission is to organize the world's information and make it universally accessible and useful.
- **General Electric:** General Electric is dedicated to turning imaginative ideas into leading products and services that help solve some of the world's toughest problems.
- **Ford Motor Company:** Ford Motor Company's mission is to become the world's leading consumer company for automotive products and services.

What do these mission statements have in common?

- They express the aspirations of the companies.
- They serve to solve a problem or improve people's lives.
- They strive to be the best at what they have to offer, refusing to settle.

Let's talk offline for a minute: I'll bet you're having one of two reactions after reading these mission statements. First, you might be motivated by how these companies strive to be the best in their field. You're probably already thinking about applying this concept to your dating approach. If that's the case, you're ahead of the game and off to a high-performing start.

It's also possible that you're having trouble relating the products and services provided by Google, General Electric, and Ford Motor Company to your quest to find a great guy. Hey, I understand where you're coming from. After all, these are multibillion-dollar companies operating in a global business environment. You're just one person, looking for love in a complex dating environment. But if we look closer, we'll see there's a lot to learn from company mission statements that can be applied to dating.

Let's think for a moment about why these companies take the time to write a mission statement. Sure it looks great to investors, and makes a statement in their annual report. But more important, the mission statement becomes a guiding light for every action taken by the company. Before Google, General Electric, or Ford targets a new customer or launches a new product, they ask whether the idea is in line with their company mission statement. In other words, will producing this product or launching this service move them closer to or further from their company vision? This is what you'll be doing when you write your Wishin' Statement. You'll create a guiding light for yourself, something you can refer to over and over again to make sure every action you take with the guys you meet is in line with your overall mission as a single woman: to be happy and find the right man for you.

···· state of the business #1 ···············
Nearly 54 percent of adult single people in the U.S. are women. So while the single guys are the minority and may appear to have their pick of the litter, hold on just one minute! Now that you'll be armed with a dating plan, the odds will shift back in your favor as you stand out from the crowd.

## Companies Don't Scribble Mission Statements on Napkins

On the surface, mission statements appear to be simple sentences. You might even think the company CEO scribbled out the company mission on a napkin and dropped it into the annual report. The reality is that mission statements look simple, but they're the final output from a carefully considered process of determining what a company truly stands for in the marketplace.

In crafting a mission statement, companies typically answer five key questions:

1. What opportunity exists in the marketplace that our company can address?
2. What can we do as a company to address this need?
3. What are the values and beliefs that guide our business?
4. Does everyone involved in our business share our philosophy?
5. How will we know when we're successful at what we do?

Napkin or no napkin, these questions take considerable thought. By the time a company settles on their official mission statement, it's been vetted by all the top executives, key employees, suppliers, and even current and potential customers. In other words, everyone involved in buying or supplying what the company has to offer is fully aware of exactly what the company is striving to accomplish. Later in this book, when we start writing your own personal Dating Business Plan, you'll see the importance of sharing your dating vision and goals with those who know you best, mainly trusted friends and family.

## The Mission Statement for *Dating, Inc.*

Okay, we've talked about Google, General Electric, and Ford Motor Company. We also broke down how companies approach writing their mission statement. Let's start getting more specific. Here's the mission statement for *Dating, Inc.*:

> *Dating, Inc.*'s mission is to teach single, successful businesswomen how to take the same business skills that help them thrive at work and apply these skills to finding and keeping a great guy.

In crafting a mission statement, we answered the five key questions as follows:

1. **What opportunity exists in the marketplace that our company can address?** Millions of women out there have achieved phenomenal success in the workplace. They're climbing the corporate ladder or starting new businesses each and every day. These dynamic women deserve the same level of success in their relationships, and *Dating, Inc.* can show them how to do it.

2. **What can we do as a company to address this need?** *Dating, Inc.* can teach single women how to apply business skills they already know, or can easily learn, to reach the same or even higher levels of success in their relationships that they currently enjoy in their careers.

3. **What are the values and beliefs that guide our business?** We believe every woman deserves a great guy and a great relationship, and nobody should ever settle, or stay in a relationship that isn't right for them because they are afraid they can't do better. We strive to motivate and encourage single women everywhere to take the values that make them all-stars at work and apply these same guiding principles to achieve their potential in relationships.

4. **Does everyone involved in our business share our philosophy?** Luckily, *Dating, Inc.* only has two employees, Carol and Jeff. We wholeheartedly and passionately believe in our philosophy. Jeff believes it from his personal success in the dating trenches, and from testimonials he's received from clients and readers that have benefited from his dating expertise. Carol believes it as a successful business woman, who has traveled this path herself.

5. **How will we know when we're successful at what we do?** We'll know we're successful when single women around the world can honestly say that their level of success in dating relationships equals their level of success at work. We'll also know we've been successful when single women no longer

rely solely on fate to find their mate. They choose to control their relationship destiny, not relying only on destiny to find a partner.

### What's Wrong With Relying on Fate to Find Your Mate?

This is a question that single men and women often ask me. Love is supposed to be emotional, so why bring in this business-oriented, logical approach to a matter of the heart? Believe me, the last thing I want you to do is start thinking of love as a business transaction. When you find that great guy, and I know you will, you'll decide with your heart whether this is the right guy for a long-term relationship. In the meantime, the business concepts taught in *Dating, Inc.* will show you a logical approach to finding and keeping great guys. This logical approach will help you meet so many great guys and feel so much confidence on the dating scene that your mind will be free to listen to your heart when it's time to think about your future with a particular guy.

## Now It's Your Turn

You've learned about company mission statements and you've read the *Dating, Inc.* mission statement. Here comes your first opportunity to translate business skills you already know into developing your own Wishin' Statement. Let's start by rewriting that e-mail from your boss and making it apply to dating.

From: your.boss@work.com
To: you@work.com
Subject: New Dating Mission
I'm off 2 a meting. Giv sum thought 2 ur dating mission.
Whut r u loooking for?
Tanks for making it happen.

If I had opened the chapter with this e-mail from your boss, it might have seemed overwhelming or intimidating. What are you looking for? That's a question you've probably been asked by your curious aunt at Thanksgiving dinner, creepy guys on the subway, and a close friend or two during a late-night instant messaging marathon.

---

## Corporate Memo

TO: All Employees
FROM: Carol Cohen
RE: Your Love Life

---

The first time I heard Jeff use the phrase "Wishin' Statement," I had to correct him. "Doesn't that run counter to the philosophy of not relying on fate when it comes to dating?" I asked. The word "wishin'" makes it sound like we're just hoping for the best!

After giving the term more thought, I realized that starting with a wish or dream is the absolute right way to go, and it's exactly how we operate at work. When someone throws a project or assignment at us, we start by visualizing the best-case scenario or what we "wish" will happen when the assignment is complete. We visualize this end goal without worrying about obstacles and challenges along the way. Instead, it's a pure process, one where we allow ourselves to think that anything is possible and know our skills will find a way to get the job done.

This same philosophy should be at the core of your Wishin' Statement. Remove the obstacles, the what-if questions, and think big. Visualize your perfect life with a great partner, someone you share everything with. Don't let self-doubt or your failed relationships dictate what's possible. Then, when that picture becomes vivid and you know what you desire in a man you can back into the action plan to make it happen.

---

The big difference now is that you're armed with the approach companies take in writing their mission statements. If Google can create a mission around their millions of customers, then I'll bet you're feeling more confident now in creating a mission for your approach to dating. Plus, if Google can use their mission to be the world's #1 search engine, there's no reason your dating mission can't skyrocket your success on the dating scene. Let's start with our definition of a Wishin' Statement.

**JEFF'S DEF•I•NI•TIONS:** According to *Dating, Inc.*, a Wishin' Statement refers to what a single woman wants to find on the dating scene, what she's looking for in a guy, or what she hopes to accomplish in a future relationship.

## The Ingredients of a Wishin' Statement

In business, you're often asked to accomplish tasks and assignments with little direction. In *Dating, Inc.* however, we try to give you as much direction as possible to make sure you are successful. So before we ask you to tackle that e-mail request and write your Wishin' Statement, here are a few exercises that can help shape your thinking:

1.  **Self Appraisal:** An honest look at your strengths and development areas when it comes to dating
2.  **Code of Conduct:** The values, beliefs, and ground rules you will hold yourself to going forward on the dating scene
3.  **Mimon Mapping:** A free-thinking dating brainstorm that can help unlock what you truly desire at your deepest, emotional levels

These three exercises together will review where you've been, set your beliefs going forward, help you look into the future, and evoke your underlying thoughts about dating. How's that for an exciting journey? Now let's get started.

## The Self–Appraisal

It's honesty time! I know this is tough. Nobody likes to examine why they might be unhappy in their relationships. If you've been hurt in the past, it can open old wounds, and in any case, it will force you to face some potentially unpleasant facts about your approach to dating. At the same time, examining your past relationships can be truly eye opening and refreshing, and it can also allow you to face the truth and move forward with confidence. The self-appraisal can give you a starting point, something to build from, and help you understand the truth about your dating success. Without that point of departure, it can be hard to make progress. But before I ask you to be honest, here are three reasons why it is imperative that you speak the truth during this exercise:

1. Nobody but yourself ever has to read what you write, so why not be honest with yourself?
2. Even if I could read what you'd write, I would never judge you for it. Instead, I'd be proud of you for facing the truth. I hope you'll feel this same pride yourself in taking this big step forward.
3. I'll bet you don't kid yourself at work—if you make a mistake, you accept it, learn from it, and move on. This is a great opportunity to apply that same honesty to your relationships to help your dating success match your work results.

At work, the point of a self-appraisal is to review your progress against goals, highlight your strengths on the job, and identify some areas of improvement. In *Dating, Inc.* we're going to make the process simpler. I only want you to answer one question about your current results in dating and relationships:

Why do you believe you've been successful at work but haven't yet found that same level of success in your relationships?

### Before You Answer, Read What Others Have to Say

Keep in mind that many women frustrated with dating have come before you—rather than reinvent the wheel when it comes to understanding relationships, why not take other people's thoughts into consideration? Did you happen to read the Acknowledgments (or reward and recognition) section of this book? If so, then you really take reading cover-to-cover seriously, and we thank you for that. You probably noticed a paragraph recognizing the smart, savvy businesswomen, businessmen, friends, and family who generously shared their business wisdom and dating war stories.

We posed this very question to our team of male and female colleagues, friends, and family. Here are the top ten answers many single, career-savvy women cited for the discrepancy between their success at work and in the relationship arena. If only one of these hits home for you or causes an "a-ha" moment, then we've done our job.

## Top Ten Reasons Single Women Are Successful on the Job But Not Yet in Love

1. **"They're too busy."** It's a self-fulfilling prophecy when a successful woman tells herself she doesn't have time for a relationship and ends up sabotaging any hope of one. In essence, her job becomes her soul mate instead of a great guy.
2. **"They can't handle not being in control."** The desire to be in control at all times can be professionally helpful, but in relationships it's a nearly impossible personality trait. This leaves single women feeling less comfortable in relationships. Being in control at work makes them happy and comfortable. Once they hit the mean streets of dating, where anything may or may not happen (and it is hard to get far without taking risks), they are way out of their comfort zones. The only way they can regain that happy and comfortable feeling is to retreat to work.
3. **"They are afraid to be vulnerable."** It's easier to have superficial and short-term relationships with men to avoid any risk of getting hurt. So, even though a woman might *say* she wants to meet someone and have a meaningful relationship, her expectations of a potential partner are all wrong. Since a woman has been successful at work, she sees relationships the same way she would getting a promotion or landing the next great account, like it's something to get done or check off her to-do list, and then move on.
4. **"They don't know how to relate to men without competing with them."** Getting a promotion or landing the next gig often requires assertiveness. But that same desire can cause women to lose their "softness" or "gentleness," qualities many men might desire in a woman. Men want a woman to complement them, not necessarily "best" them.

5. **"They sabotage building a relationship with someone by having sex with them too soon."** Some women get too physical too fast, and that may prevent them from forming a relationship and getting to really know somebody. This is an aggressiveness that helps on the job but can backfire in relationships.

6. **"They date down."** There is a tendency by some women to try to date the person that the guy could be, should be, or wants to be, rather than who he is. At work, women can give feedback to male direct reports to change their behaviors, but this does not work as well in relationships.

7. **"They're so 'over it!'"** Many women are dinosaurs in the dating game. They're sick of the games and sick of dating. They want the right guy to just magically show up so they can get married. This game playing is easier to stamp out at work by eliminating politics in the office. It's much tougher to get rid of the game playing in relationships.

8. **"Men can't handle their success."** Great women, those who are successful at work and have killer personalities, are very confident in dating as well. Unfortunately, sometimes this same quality can come across as intimidating to men and if so, it scares them off.

9. **"The stakes are too high and too personal."** There is a clear reward system at work: You work hard, and you get rewarded (with a bonus, or a promotion, something nice). In dating, even if you work hard, you don't always see the positive outcomes, and the failures are harder to overcome, so people give up too quickly.

10. **"They're hypercritical and overanalytical."** Overevaluating and overanalyzing are important qualities at work, but they get single women in trouble in their relationships. It makes men think they're not secure in the relationship. It's okay to be ambitious at work, but in relationships you can't overanalyze every word spoken, every facial expression, and every inflection of his voice.

## Corporate Memo

TO: All Employees
FROM: Carol Cohen
RE: Your Love Life

Every item on that list either describes how I've thought about dating or represents how some of the most confident, know-how businesswomen I've worked with approach dating. I'll bet you might even see some of yourself in the list too. Promise me you won't beat yourself up if at one point you've heard yourself saying one, or even several items on that list. This book is not about feeling bad about yourself! It's about learning and "up-skilling" when it comes to success in your dating approach, in the same way you learn new skills or strategies at work to do your job more successfully. Remember, trust in the knowledge that we're SuperStars at work, and we can be SuperStars in our relationships, too. Draw strength and encouragement from the self-awareness and honesty in that list. After all, at the heart of the list are examples from other people supporting your success by sharing their insights and lessons learned! So don't be afraid to admit to a few items on the list. Better yet, laugh at it because at least you know you're not alone in feeling this way. The more honest you are now, the better your results will be later in applying the strategies in this book.

### Now It's Your Turn

You just read ten honest comments from ten people about why single women succeed at the office but sometimes struggle in relationships. Now I want you to look at the list again and circle the ones that might apply to you. Remember, nobody will ever see this, so be honest (unless you loan this book to a friend, then all bets are off!).

Now that you've circled one or more items, use the space on the following page to list as many as three additional reasons that you believe might be holding you back in dating. My network is good, but I doubt they described you spot-on. So round out the reasons above with some additional thoughts. Remember, the key here is to write insights about your personal dating approach in your self appraisal that may be preventing you from having the same success in dating as you do in work:

**1.** _____

_____

**2.** _____

_____

**3.** _____

_____

### *A Little Motivational Reward and Recognition Goes a Long Way*

Let me be the first to congratulate you for your honesty. I know it wasn't easy. You probably stared at a few items on that list for several minutes before you summoned the courage to admit they apply to you. I promise that if *Dating, Inc.* ever organizes an off-site meeting, we'll conduct a reward and recognition ceremony. You'll be honored, your fellow attendees will cheer feverishly, you'll whisk your way on stage to collect a glass sculpture, and you'll deliver a thank-you speech leaving not a dry eye in the house. Until Carol and I organize that off-site, at the very least pat yourself on the back for a job well done. Also, be sure to keep the items you circled and the add-on thoughts handy because they will be used later in this chapter when you formulate your Wishin' Statement.

### *Zero-Tolerance Policy*

As you can tell, this whole chapter is all about honesty. You've got to be honest with what's holding you back and honest with what you want going forward in a relationship. Speaking of honesty, here's Joel's candid take on setting high standards when it comes to looking for the right person. (Remember how we told you some of the male members of our SuperStar Network just couldn't help but chime in? Well, this is one of those times). Joel is a thirty-six-year-old software programmer from Seattle, Washington:

*"You are worth a lot and deserve the best. If someone repeatedly fails to live up to your expectations, you cut them loose and find someone who will. That person is out there, you need to be patient. What I see happen a lot is people get into relationships and little things start to bother them about the people they are dating, but they figure that they can deal with it. The problem is that if something bothers you about a person a little during the first month or two of dating, it's going to aggravate you by six months and become a deal breaker after a year. At that point, resentment has built but the person has been exhibiting the behavior for a year now so it's hard to talk about getting them to change. This isn't absolute, obviously you have to let some things go in relationships—but you need to take the time to know yourself well so you'll know what your boundaries are and what constitutes a deal breaker. Trust yourself to not settle, and remove yourself from bad situations when they arise."*

## Your Dating Code of Conduct

Now that you found that honest place, it's time to hold yourself to a new standard. Remember, you deserve a great guy and setting the right personal standards, including a zero-tolerance policy for behavior that doesn't cut it, is a great starting place. Companies go beyond their mission statement to include a code of conduct in their business planning and annual reports. The code of conduct represents a set of standards by which all actions, decisions, and behaviors will be guided. If you've ever seen a movie with a military theme, then you're probably already familiar with codes of conduct.

So let's start by thinking about setting those new standards. What are some new standards you could follow in improving your dating results? Here are a few suggestions, tried-and-true basics that you should always bear in mind:

1. I will not let my past history in dating dictate my future results.
2. I deserve to achieve the same level of success in dating that I have in my career.

**3.** I will not settle if the wrong guy comes along. I'd rather be single and actively looking than in an unhappy committed relationship.

You can incorporate some or all of the previous ideas into your code of conduct. Reflect on the standards you want to set for yourself. If you have new ones to add to the previous list, write down your thoughts here:

**1.** _____

_____

**2.** _____

_____

**3.** _____

_____

---

## Corporate Memo

TO: All Employees
FROM: Carol Cohen
RE: Your Love Life

---

Think about how you carry yourself at work, with poise and professionalism. I'll bet a personal code of conduct is at the very heart of everything you do, and that you have a set of personal standards for how you deal with customers, how you interact with your boss, and how you treat direct reports. You probably even have a personal code of conduct in your own work ethic, one that drives you to keep your eye on the goal and get the job done when the pressure is on. You have standards for yourself with coworkers, clients, even strangers who you interact with in your everyday business life. Shouldn't you have something similar when it comes to dating? For example, I'm sure you'd never act combative on a first meeting with a client, or dominate conversation during an important business lunch, even if you were feeling a bit nervous. Would you avoid the same behaviors on a first date? And at work, if a particular vendor wasn't listening to or responding to your company's needs, you definitely wouldn't continue working with them! Would you draw the same boundary if you found yourself wrapped up with a guy who had a similar problem?

There's nothing stopping successful women like us from understanding the standards by which we live, and translating them into the way we conduct ourselves on the dating scene. It will keep our eye on the prize, prevent us from settling for guys who aren't up to snuff, and eventually land us in the right relationship. The code of conduct that drives your success at work will lead to the same outstanding results in your relationships.

---

### Women's Intuition

As you write all these great goals and headlines, you'll move closer and closer to finding that great guy. But what will you do once you find this guy? Here's Melissa's take on how your SuperStar behavior at work can translate effectively in relationships. Melissa is thirty-one. She lives in Detroit and has spent the last four years running a small boutique store:

*"Being motivated, organized, and energetic is the key to success! I think many people put way more energy into their work lives than into their personal relationships. Using that same motivation to do a great job at work can help you do a great job being a life partner. Relationships don't just run themselves. Anticipating needs; trying to impress; putting your best self forward; seeming positive even when you don't feel that positive about a situation; compromising and working as a team; treating others with respect—these are the things we all do at work, but I think some people treat their coworkers with more respect than their relationship partners."*

## Mimon Mapping

You've done the self-appraisal to find that honest place and crafted your Code of Conduct. You've written a few headlines to get your dating vision flowing. Now it's time for one last exercise before you craft your Wishin' Statement: the Mimon Map.

You may be familiar with the better-known term, Mind Map. Created in the late 1960s by Tony Buzan, Mind Maps are an illustrative technique used to unleash the deepest thinking and desires in your brain.

You start with a blank piece of paper, write a challenge or problem in the middle of the paper, and circle it. Then, without editing or stopping yourself, write down all the thoughts and ideas you can think of related to that word, circling each thought, and connecting them like spokes on a bicycle. Afterward, you go back and review your work. Themes will emerge from your free-flowing thinking that may give you insights into what you really desire in tackling the challenge or problem.

---

### Corporate Memo

TO: All Employees
FROM: Carol Cohen
RE: Your Love Life

At work, budgeting and forecasting are regular parts of many people's job. At the beginning of the year, we make predictions about things like revenue, net income, and expenses. We then spend the year working toward those target numbers.

Writing a Dating Business Plan for your relationships requires the same skills. Rather than sit back and just let your relationships play out based on fate, why not think and plan ahead of time? This is your future we're talking about—if it's good enough for your company, it's good enough for you! Similar to forecasting a budget in your work life, you make predictions about what you want to see happen in your love life. Then you spend the year working toward making those predictions come true. Mark my words: your odds of success will go up. They do on the job—who's to say they won't in your personal life?

---

### What's the Difference Between Mind Mapping and Mimon Mapping?

There is no difference. Carol's maiden name is Mimon, and we wanted her to feel connected to her origins. Additionally, Carol uses Mind Mapping all the time on the job and in her personal life to find themes, create clarity, and provide insight into her real thoughts on many of life's biggest challenges.

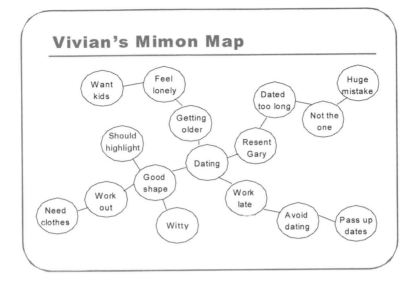

## Vivian's Mimon Map

(Want kids) (Feel lonely) (Dated too long) (Huge mistake)
(Getting older) (Not the one)
(Should highlight) (Resent Gary)
(Dating)
(Good shape)
(Work out) (Work late)
(Need clothes) (Avoid dating) (Pass up dates)
(Witty)

So how can you use Mimon Mapping to help in crafting your Wishin' Statement? Well, the self-appraisal focused on honest Mimon Mapping will unlock those subconscious thoughts that only come out when you don't edit yourself.

Your job is to start with "dating" written in the center of a blank page and circle it. We've done this for you already to get you started (see page 23).

Before you jump into your own Mimon Map, let's bring this concept to life. Here's Vivian's Mimon Map. She's a thirty-four-year-old director at a retail company in Chicago. Vivian dated Gary for seven years. The couple reached a comfortable place with each other, but neither of them ever pushed the relationship forward toward marriage. Eventually Vivian and Gary felt more like brother and sister than boyfriend and girlfriend. The relationship finally ended two years ago and Vivian has dated sporadically ever since. Let's check out Vivian's Mimon Map.

Let's analyze Vivian's Mimon Map for a moment. What themes emerge? Clearly there are some pent-up feelings about her relationship with Gary. It seems like Vivian believes she missed a dating window by staying with Gary so long. When we pointed this out to Vivian while discussing her map, she agreed. "I realized from my Mimon Map shortly after we broke up that the seven years I spent with him left me in my mid-thirties, feeling lonely for someone new, and wondering when—sometimes even *if*—I'll have kids. In a way, I feel angry with both of us, for letting things go on at a mediocre pace for so long." Vivian also admitted that in the years since she and Gary broke up, working late has caused her to avoid dating and in many cases pass up opportunities to meet eligible men. On the plus side, Vivian feels good about her body. " I like to stay in shape, it's something I do for myself, and that makes me feel confident and sexy when I do find myself in the presence of a hot guy." From Vivian's map, it seems like a wardrobe makeover could do the trick to match her clothing to how she feels about her body. Vivian also recognizes that she has a great sense of humor, and after drawing her Mimon Map, she felt motivated to accentuate that part of her personality. "I may even take a stand-up comedy class on the side—who knows, maybe that will be the place where I meet my dream guy. At the very least, I'm sure it will be a lot of fun."

Keep in mind that this is a simplified Mimon Map. The point here is to demonstrate how the process works and show you the insights that can come from it. You'll likely have more words, circles, and spokes. Just remember, the more you create, the more insights you'll find about your dating desires, So if you find yourself circling and spoking like nobody's business, then you're doing this exercise right! So now it's your turn—let's see what you come up with.

Dating

### Let's Recap Your Mimon Map

Who better than Carol to help you interpret your Mimon Map? After all, it is her maiden name. Carol will ask you some insightful questions to help you make the most of your results.

---

## Corporate Memo

TO: All Employees
FROM: Carol Cohen
RE: Your Love Life

---

Okay ladies, what did you come up with? Here are some questions you should ask yourself about your Mimon Map.

1.  What themes emerged that bring a smile to your face or add confidence to your thoughts on dating? Do you love your BCBG suits and your sassy, sexy haircut? Or your cheeky sense of humor and ability to make compelling conversation?

2.  Where did you see things that might be holding you back or preventing you from moving forward in finding a great guy? Are you working too many late nights while your girlfriends are out meeting men, like Vivian?

3.  What fears or uncertainties came through? How can you tackle them now before they get in the way of the next great guy who comes your way? Do you feel too insecure or sheepish about something that your discomfort about it is palpable, and possibly driving away great guys?

4.  What went well in previous relationships that you want to learn from and be sure to carry over into your future relationships? Have you always been a good listener for your exes? Have you motivated men in your past to reach their potential?

5.  What surprised you about your Mimon Map? How can you use this surprising information in crafting your Wishin' Statement? Did any themes emerge that surprised you?

Once you've answered the five questions above, spend some time tapping into your own intellectual curiosity. Reflect on the Mimon Map and ask yourself what else jumps out at you? You may just unlock your own potential.

## Let's Put It All Together Now

You've got your self-appraisal, Code of Conduct, and Mimon Map. Now you're officially ready to put it all together into your Wishin' Statement. Think of the exercises you just completed as the foundation to writing a Wishin' Statement that's right for you. As a reminder from Jeff's Defs, the Wishin' Statement refers to what a single woman wants to find on the dating scene or hopes to accomplish in a future relationship.

So your job is to piece together your self-appraisal, your Code of Conduct, and what you've learned from your Mimon Map to create your own Wishin' Statement. But if you know Carol and me by now, then you know we would never ask you to complete a Wishin' Statement without providing a few samples to support and motivate you. So check out these sample Wishin' Statements and see if you can use any of the material to get ideas for yourself.

### Sample #1—Jennifer, 28
Advertising Executive from Denver, Colorado

I love that football player build, pure muscle and some meat on those bones. There's something about a bulky guy that just makes me feel protected. I don't even mind if he's a little cocky, I see that as a sign of confidence.

I want the guy to be close to his family, but not so close that they make decisions for him. I've got to come first and when we have a family, he should put our family first. The guy better understand that I want a career too. If he expects me to give it all up to raise the kids, he's with the wrong woman.

Chemistry between the sheets is huge. If he's selfish in bed or doesn't know how to please a woman, we've got problems. After all, I'm giving up every other single guy in the universe for him; he better know or be willing to learn how to push my buttons.

### Sample #2—Jill, 48
High School Teacher from Cleveland, Ohio

I can get emotional sometimes; I need a really patient guy. If he can't handle me getting worked up here and there, it's not going to work. I don't care how tall he is, brown or blue eyes don't matter, and he can even have a potbelly. It's all about how he treats me.

I like to live comfortably, so I hope this guy is ambitious. I'm not looking for him to work ninety hours per week, but a nice house and some fun vacations would be nice. I'm a teacher, and I love doing it, but it doesn't exactly make you rich.

I'll admit it, I take a puff here and there. I'd like to quit smoking, but haven't been successful yet. So I guess I'm up for a smoker too, or at least someone who will help me quit.

### Sample #3—Sharon, 36
Web Designer from Montreal, Canada

I know instantly if I'm attracted to a guy, so his looks are really important. If I'm not instantly attracted, it will never work.

I like to spend a lot of time with my guy, so I don't want any work-aholics or guys who need "guys night out" every other evening. If he doesn't want to cuddle up with me and watch a movie, we won't last.

Oh yeah, have some hygiene. I can't stand dirty fingernails, any unusual odors, or guys who won't shower after a workout.

### Sample #4—Juanita, 39
Freelance Writer from Queens, New York

I'd like to find a person that I can be myself around. I want to encourage them to be the person they can be and have them do that for me. If we can make each other laugh, I'm sold. I'm kind of a homebody so party types need not apply. I'm looking for a serious relationship at this point. A true partner.

Let's talk offline for a minute: I'm going to be really honest with you. I would never pretend to know what your Wishin' Statement should look like. Every single woman is different, and that means there's a Wishin' Statement unique to every single woman's dating desires. So feel free to use some of these samples for a few ideas or completely disregard them. The important thing is that when you read your own Wishin' Statement, it should bring a smile to your face. That means you have described the exact guy you're looking for. If you can do that, then you are well on your way to making your Wishin' Statement a reality.

## It's Wishin' Time

You've read the definition and seen the samples—now it's your turn. Once again, the more honesty the better. Carol and I would never judge you for your Wishin' Statement. This is a picture of your ideal type and you have every right to stand by your description. Now let's get to work. In the space provided, write out your Wishin' Statement. By the way, if you prefer, instead of using this space, you can complete your Wishin' Statement in Appendix 1 of this book. That way, you'll have the option of building your overall Dating Business Plan in one place rather than in chunks or segments throughout the book. Everyone has their own style, so I wanted to give you options to help get you on the journey one way or another. The choice is yours.

_____

_____

_____

_____

_____

## It's Reward Time Again

Before you continue reading, take a minute and congratulate yourself. You've just taken your first big step in applying a business principle to finding a great guy. You've taken the business concept of a mission statement and applied it to your Wishin' Statement. You've already proven to be the super-smart woman I knew you were all along by successfully applying a business concept to your love life. I'll bet it wasn't too hard after all. The good news is that I promise it will get easier and easier to make the translation as the chapters unfold.

### Women's Intuition

Speaking of reward and recognition, this is a concept that translates really well from work to relationships. Here's Barrie's take on how reward and recognition in the office applies to relationships. Barrie is a nurse practitioner with clients spread throughout New York and New Jersey:

"A pat on the back goes a long way at work and in relationships. I find both in relationships and at work that appreciation and acknowledgment are real morale boosters and that they instill respect and positive attitudes toward one another. No one likes to be taken for granted, and I feel recognition is essential for relationships to stand the test of time. I'm not talking about anything elaborate here, although that can be nice every once in a while, too. In many cases, just a simple thank you can do the job."

## Sneak Preview

Now that you have a Wishin' Statement in place, it's time to move on to your Souls and Objectives. As we said in our opening remarks, for savvy single women like you, Souls and Objectives complement the Wishin' Statement by drilling deeper. If a Wishin' Statement envisions landing a husband, then the Souls and Objectives would describe the man's character, his personality, his appearance, and his profession. The Souls and Objectives bring the abstract Wishin' Statement to life. That's what you'll be doing as we move forward together to Principle #2.

## The Bottom Line

You're ready to move on to the next chapter if all the following are true:

- You know why companies create mission statements and the role they play in an organization.
- You understand how a mission statement in business translates to a Wishin' Statement in dating and relationships.
- You created your own code of conduct to guide you going forward in your approach to dating.
- You completed your self-appraisal, headlines, and Mimon Map to review your past, aspire for the future, and unlock your hidden dating desires.
- You created your own Wishin' Statement and feel it accurately describes the type of guy you desire.

# chapter **two**

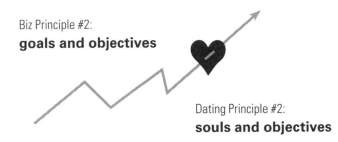

Biz Principle #2:
**goals and objectives**

Dating Principle #2:
**souls and objectives**

## Agenda

- How mission statements funnel into goals and objectives
- How goals and objectives in business translate into Souls and Objectives in dating
- The difference between must-have, nice-to-have, and who-cares qualities
- Why goals without timelines and milestones are rarely met
- Developing personal dating metrics or targets to monitor your success

## Work/Life Balance

You're back at your desk after a ten-minute meeting to discuss that ad-hoc assignment with your boss. It's now 9:21 A.M. It's been eleven minutes since you put down the coffee, and amazingly, fourteen new e-mails have hit your inbox. It's going to be one of those days.

Scanning the new arrivals, there are thirteen business-related e-mails and one personal e-mail from your old college roommate. The subject line says, "Important Mind Twister." You're eager to tackle your boss's assignment, and you know you'll do a great job, but you can't resist challenging the mind twister. You launch the e-mail and see a word jumble consisting of four words. The ad-hoc project can wait five minutes while you unscramble the word jumble.

## TGE FOF TEH SSIEDNELI _____

How did you do? Here's a little hint. Think about a place that fans at a sporting event typically sit. Still stuck? There's always the back of the book and the answer key. Once you unscramble this word jumble, you'll have the most important message for this chapter. You'll know something that you simply must do if you want to accomplish your dating goals and score a great guy.

---

### Corporate Memo

---

TO: All Employees
FROM: Carol Cohen
RE: Your Love Life

---

Without giving away the word jumble (I'm pretty sure you solved it by now anyway), I want to emphasize the importance of taking action in goal setting. At work, we would never set a goal with no intention of following through and making it happen. It's the action plan, timelines, and milestones that make sure our goals are on track for delivery.

As we start talking about goal setting, definitely keep that business mindset. I know your dating goals will feel more emotional, complicated, and scary than launching a new product or rolling out a new service. That's precisely why I want to remind you that it's your same go-getter attitude and positive mentality that will serve you well as we begin laying out your dating goals. You can do it at the office, right? And isn't your personal happiness as important as your professional success?

---

# Goal Away

Sometimes we all wish goals would just go away. Wouldn't it be nice to lounge on a hammock, sipping piña coladas, as the gentle breeze of the ocean drifts past your perfectly tanned body? Life would seem so simple. Unfortunately, very few people achieve the piña-colada, gentle-breeze scenario without setting goals and going after them. So instead of wishing goals would just go away, it's time to adopt a new slogan: "Goal Away." This new slogan will represent your commitment to getting off the sidelines of life and making your own action.

## What Exactly Are Goals and Objectives?

Before we break down the process of setting goals and objectives, let's start simply with the basic definition.

> **JEFF'S DEF•I•NI•TIONS:** According to the Society for Human Resource Management, goals are statements outlining the long-term results, accomplishments, or objectives an organization seeks to attain. Objectives are a specification of what is to be accomplished, the timeframe in which it is to be accomplished, and by whom.

The corporate goal-setting process typically includes five key steps:

1. **Mission review:** How can a company ensure every established goal works in conjunction with the mission statement?
2. **Goal statements:** What are the specific actions a company wants to take in the coming year to achieve its mission?

3. **Timelines:** What timeframe will be established for achieving each of the goal statements?
4. **Milestones:** Are there specific events or actions a company can take along the way to know they're on track for reaching their goals?
5. **Success measures:** What quantitative and qualitative metrics can be established to measure the positive impact of a company's goal achievements?

Look, I know this is a dating and relationship book. The last thing I want to do is bore you with a full breakdown of the goal-setting process in an organization. How about we compromise here? I'll make it easy for you and give just one simple example to illustrate. Then we can get right back to dating and relationships. This will just take a minute. I promise.

### Goal Setting at General Electric

Do you remember General Electric's Mission statement from Chapter 1? Hmmm, should I make you flip back and find it or write it again here? If I write it here again, do you promise to back me up if my editors think I'm being repetitive? It's a deal.

> "General Electric's mission is to turn imaginative ideas into leading products and services that help solve some of the world's toughest problems."

How might General Electric complete these five steps? Let's take a quick tour through the five stages of goal setting to see the process in action.

1. **Mission review:** This could be as simple as writing the company Mission Statement at the top of the goal-setting page. It will serve as a constant reminder that every goal written should work toward, not against, the company mission.
2. **Goal statements:** Let's keep this example simple and stick to one goal. Let's say General Electric wants to create a new light bulb that lasts twice as long as their current models.

3. **Timelines:** You might think that only one deadline matters here, the date General Electric wants to roll this new light bulb out to the public. That's an important deadline, but other dates matter too. Examples might include a deadline for designing the new light bulb, creating sales collateral to attract customers, and testing the light bulb before it goes to market.

4. **Milestones:** Rather than just think about successfully creating the new light bulb, General Electric would likely set key milestones along the way to make sure the light bulb launch is on track. Examples might include establishing a budget to design the light bulb and cutting deals with retail stores to stock and sell the new light bulb.

5. **Success measures:** Quantitative metrics that indicate a successful product might include the number of light bulbs sold in a year. Qualitative metrics might include customer satisfaction with the new product.

## Corporate Memo

TO: All Employees
FROM: Carol Cohen
RE: Your Love Life

As savvy businesswomen, we definitely know the goal-setting process can sometimes be more complex than Jeff's example. The key idea here is that our mentality of setting goals and going after them is something that makes us incredibly successful on the job. Think about it. At work, we set the goal, establish a timeline, generate milestones, and track our success. We always know at work how we're doing against our goals. Why can't we apply the same logic to dating? We absolutely should be! Again, we're not talking about viewing dating as a business transaction. But we can certainly think about dating in terms of achieving a goal rather than passively sitting back and hoping for the best.

## Let's Get to the Business of Dating

From: your.boss@work.com
To: you@work.com
Subject: Souls and Objectives
I'm running late. we needd to starrt tinking about ur dating goals.
Tanks for making it happen.

This just in! Your boss now wants you to think about your dating goals. At work, I'll bet you've written countless goals, but have you ever written a dating goal? Hey, if you can write a goal to launch a new product, there's no reason you can't write a goal to meet a great guy.

Now, you might think that since *meeting* a great guy is your main goal, you might as well breeze on through to Chapter 3. I'll give you two reasons why that would be a mistake:

1.  While meeting a great guy may be your main goal, it's not specific enough to take action on. Think about it—at work, would you ever just say, "My goal is to be CEO," and consider your job done? In both cases, a goal like this won't fly!

2.  When we decided to write this book, we had to write it cover to cover to make sure we set you up for success. So it's only fair that you read it cover to cover, too.

Take a journey with us through the goal-setting process. I promise that by the time you finish the five steps, you'll have a crystal-clear picture of the guy you want to meet.

> **JEFF'S DEF•I•NI•TIONS:** According to *Dating, Inc.*, the "Souls" part of "Souls and Objectives" are statements outlining the long-term results, accomplishments, or objectives a single woman seeks to attain in her relationships. Objectives are a specification of what is to be accomplished, the timeframe in which it is to be accomplished, and by whom (in case you're wondering, "whom" refers to YOU).

You've got the definition of Souls and Objectives, and you know the five steps an organization would take to achieve its goals. Now let's apply this very practical business skill to your approach in dating.

## Step 1: Mission Review (or should we say Wishin' Review?)

Do you remember that Wishin' Statement masterpiece you wrote in Chapter 1? Now's the time to look at it again. So save this page with your thumb, bookmark, pretzel, or whatever else you can get your hands on. First, read the Wishin' Statement to make sure it definitely sounds like you. If we're going to go on this journey together, I want you to know in your heart that accomplishing your Wishin' Statement would truly make you happy. That's what this whole process is all about. Second, keep your Wishin' Statement handy throughout this chapter because every goal you set should get you closer to your Wishin' Statement. If any of your goals run counter to your Wishin' Statement, then there's either a problem with the goal or your Wishin' Statement.

### What's the Difference Between a Wishin' Statement and a Goal?

In business, there's often confusion between a vision and a goal. In fact, sometimes both use similar language. Think back to Jeff's Defs. The Wishin' Statement refers to what a single woman wants to find on the dating scene or hopes to accomplish in a future relationship. Souls and Objectives are goals and statements outlining the long-term results or objectives a single woman seeks to attain. Think of it as the "What" and the "How." Your Wishin' Statement is "what" you hope to achieve, and the Souls and Objectives are "How" you will get there. So the Souls and Objectives basically bring the abstract Wishin' Statement to life.

### Soul Statements

By now you're officially ready to dive into writing your dating goals, or soul statements. But before you do, I want to help get you there by introducing a concept called must-have, nice-to-have, and who-cares. Think about the person you envisioned in your Wishin' Statement. Really try to see him. Bring him to life in your mind.

Wait a minute. Did you just jump to this paragraph without really visualizing the guy? Remember, we're on the honor system here. It's not like I can stand over you while you're reading and make sure you actually do the exercises. Let's try this one more time. Take that time to really make sure you can see a visual of the guy. Okay, now you've got that mental image. Let's continue.

As you visualize this guy, it's natural to start thinking about the guy's character, his personality, his appearance, and his profession. Is he tall, dark, and handsome? Rich, smart, and funny? It's this vision that helps bring the guy to life. However, as you start adding more qualities to your man, there comes a point where you have to decide which qualities are the deal breakers, which you hope he'll have, and which don't really matter. This is where the must-have, nice-to-have, and who-cares philosophy comes in.

## Corporate Memo

TO: All Employees
FROM: Carol Cohen
RE: Your Love Life

Think of the must-have, nice-to-have, and who-cares philosophy like a negotiation at work. As businesswomen, many of us have faced negotiations with customers and suppliers or seen a colleague working on a business deal. We go into the negotiation with a laundry list of what we want. Our wants are often categorized into three areas: negotiating points that must be agreed to or we'll walk away from the deal, points that we hope to accomplish but won't make or break the deal, and points that we don't care how they play out.

In fact, a former colleague of mine who still conducts many negotiations has this advice: "First you have to make sure both parties are ready and willing to negotiate. If one party isn't interested in engaging in a negotiation, there is no reason to continue. The main goal is to strike a deal so that both parties are satisfied. In both work and relationships you need to go into the negotiation knowing what your parameters are. Essentially, you need to know exactly what you are looking to accomplish; what you are willing to forfeit and what concessions you are able to make . . . without it, there is no way you will leave the negotiation feeling good about the arrangement."

We can apply this same negotiating approach to describing our ideal mate. For example, maybe being a nonsmoker is a must-have quality, a specific religion is a nice-to-have, and political party affiliation is a who-cares. By breaking down the qualities into these three buckets, you can narrow in on what you really want in a guy. This type of clarity and straightforward approach will help you reach your ultimate dating goals.

## Smart, Savvy Samples

If you know Carol and me by now, then you know we'd never ship you off to write your own must-have, nice-to-have, who-cares list without some extra guidance. So we went right to the source and asked three single, successful women for their lists.

### Meet Alyson

Alyson is a successful defense attorney and civil litigator. She's never met a plaintiff she couldn't break down with laser-sharp questioning and superior analytical skills. Alyson is best described as a "serial monogamist." She goes from one boyfriend to the next, each relationship lasting six months to a year before the inevitable breakup. Alyson is ready to surpass that one-year milestone and find the right guy. When it comes to qualities she seeks, here's what Alyson had to say:

> **Must-have:** Intelligent, college educated, attractive, easy to talk to, as tall as or taller than me (I like to wear heels), strong drive to succeed, wants children, wise with money.
> **Nice-to-have:** Same religion, likes working out, good fashion sense, makes good money.
> **Who-cares:** Hair color, eye color (to be honest, not much falls into my who-cares category)!

### Meet Cathy

Cathy works for a nonprofit organization in Seattle. Long ago, she made a self-liberating choice and decided to pick passion over money. Cathy knows she could be a great salesperson or account manager, but she willingly chose to funnel her energy into helping troubled youth. On the dating front, Cathy recently broke up with a guy after five years together. She'll readily admit the breakup happened about four years too late. Now that she's back out there, here's what Cathy is looking for:

> **Must-have:** Ambition, passion, experience in the world, respect for me, good relationship with his family, good friends, makes me laugh, kind, self-confident, liked by my friends and family.
> **Nice-to-have:** Good looks, youthful spirit, a gentleman, likes animals, good taste in music, willing to try new things.
> **Who-cares:** Material wealth, sexual prowess.

### *Meet Leslie*

Leslie works for an international bank and is currently on assignment in London. In nine years at the bank, she's worked in New York, San Francisco, Barcelona, and now London. The globetrotting has been great for her career but challenging for finding a quality guy. Here's Leslie's list (and let's just say she really knows what she wants):

> **Must-have:** Physical attraction (whether it's at first sight or just someone's looks grow on you when their personality shines through), being compatible on different levels (background, sexually, personality traits, lifestyles), chemistry (the initial spark or butterflies when you think of or see that person), being a supportive and understanding friend, someone who can maintain the right level of independence without cutting the other person out of their lives (for instance, *not* looking for someone married to his job), someone who knows what they want, mature enough not to be a time waster, sense of humor about himself, never takes himself too seriously but humble and not boastful.
> **Nice-to-have:** Sociable, adaptable and resourceful to new environments and situations, some ambition and sense of adventure, a certain admirable talent that makes them rise above the rest, self-sufficiency, frank and good at giving a nonjudgmental objective perspective, someone who will help you keep your feet on the ground, content with life and what it's got to offer, makes the most of what they've got, perceptive

and sensitive to other's feelings, has nice friends and family you can relate to.

**Who-cares:** Has different interests, can be happy with just sharing some interests but can enjoy them in own time too, success and money, perfect physique, doubtful past (baggage doesn't bother me as long as they've moved on and learned from it), past or present failures (as long as they can show they are able to bounce back).

### Women's Intuition

You can't talk qualities and traits without thinking about strengths and weaknesses. Every guy, no matter how great he is, will come with some less-than-likeable traits. Thanks to Angelica, a speech pathologist in Florida, here's how she recognized the very common business phrase "core competencies" should be applied to dating and relationships:

"Find out what each person is good at and leverage those strengths instead of only trying to get your partner to overcome whatever weakness you may think he or she may have. In business terms, the core competencies are those things that a company does best. I honestly believe in a relationship you have to understand what each partner does best and for each of you to bring out and enhance those qualities in each other. If you know your partner is a horrible multitasker, don't get angry at him or her for not remembering to set up a dental appointment and pick up the dry-cleaning at the same time. Talk and find out what each person likes to do, and come to a middle ground. My boyfriend may be more nurturing than me because that's his strength, where I am better at maintaining the personal finances and keeping our schedules on track. Focus on those strengths! Don't spend all your energies trying to change someone to overcome his or her weaknesses. It only wastes time and effort and may even backfire in the end. Work with what you have and make it even better!"

···**state of the business #2** ···············
Over the last thirty years, the median age for women to get married in the United States alone has increased by five years. So if you're still on the prowl for Mr. Right, don't get discouraged. Your counterparts are also waiting longer than before to walk down the aisle.

## Corporate Memo

TO: All Employees
FROM: Carol Cohen
RE: Your Love Life

Success at work can be defined in a lot of different ways for women. We might desire money, power, passion for our jobs, work/life balance. Only we can answer what would truly make us happy on the job.

Understanding success in relationships is the exact same self-defined thing. As you look at Alyson, Cathy, and Leslie's must-have, nice-to-have, and who-cares lists, you see they paint very different pictures. It's important to be honest in dating and really figure out what would make *you* happy. You wouldn't go after a goal at work if deep down you knew it ran counter to your career plans. Similarly, all your dating energy should go into finding the guy who meets your desired description.

## Now It's Your Turn to Give It a Whirl

You've read three examples from three successful women. Now it's your turn to identify your own must-have, nice-to-have, and who-cares qualities. Here at *Dating, Inc.* we try to make things as easy as possible. Business is all about identifying efficiencies and process improvements to achieve your goals, so why not do the same in this book?

To help you narrow in on the qualities you desire, here's a list of sample characteristics to consider as you start your own list. Some you'll find very important, others somewhat important, and others you won't care about as much.

The goal here is to figure out which qualities are must-haves, which qualities are nice-to-haves, and which qualities you couldn't care less about. The must-have qualities will be the ones you definitely incorporate into your description of the ideal guy when we write your dating goals later in this chapter.

For each characteristic, put a check mark in the box that indicates your preference. Then at the bottom of the chart, add up the total checks for each column to get your score.

It might help here if you try to visualize that future person you want to be with. Close your eyes, lean back in your chair and bring this guy to life. Or even reminisce about the better qualities of your ex-boyfriends. Either way, you're keeping your eye on the prize and that's what this chart is all about. As a reminder, you can fill in this chart either right here or in the back of the book if you prefer to keep your entire Dating Business Plan in one place. Also, if you need a little more help before you complete your chart, skip ahead to the next page for a sample, completed chart.

### Must-Have/Nice-to-Have/Who-Cares Chart

| Characteristic | Your Preference/Description | Must Have | Nice to Have | Who Cares |
|---|---|---|---|---|
| **Physical Traits** Eye Color Hair Color Height Weight Body Type Age Range Other | | | | |
| **Descriptive Traits** Race Religion Smoking Drinking Pets Education Career Other | | | | |
| **Intangible Traits** Ambition Patience Sense of Humor Communication Listening Skills Sexual Chemistry Family Closeness Desire for Kids Other | | | | |
| **Total Checks** | | | | |

Lisa works at a large financial services firm in midtown Manhattan, has a hard-earned M.B.A., and is currently eyeing her first vice president role. On the dating front, Lisa doesn't get out much and has skipped many a date for bleary-eyed late nights on the job. Recently, Lisa has decided to put that same energy she gives to her corporate life into her love life. Here's her chart.

### Lisa's Must-Have/Nice-to-Have/Who-Cares Chart

| Characteristic | Your Preference/Description | Must Have | Nice to Have | Who Cares |
|---|---|---|---|---|
| **Physical Traits** | | | | |
| Eye Color | Love baby brown eyes | ✓ | | |
| Hair Color | Don't care | | | ✓ |
| Height | At least 5' 8", I like to wear heels | ✓ | | |
| Weight | A little belly is okay with me | | ✓ | |
| Body Type | No preference | | | ✓ |
| Age Range | Over 25, younger than my dad | ✓ | | |
| Other | | | | |
| **Descriptive Traits** | | | | |
| Race | Prefer my own race | ✓ | | |
| Religion | Open to all religions | | | ✓ |
| Smoking | Smokers discouraged | | ✓ | |
| Drinking | Couple of drinks never hurt anyone | | ✓ | |
| Pets | I'm allergic to cats, dogs only | | ✓ | |
| Education | College education | ✓ | | |
| Career | Steady job | ✓ | | |
| Finances | Can support himself | | ✓ | |
| Other | | | | |
| **Intangible Traits** | | | | |
| Ambition | Doesn't have to run for President | | ✓ | |
| Patience | Would be nice | | ✓ | |
| Sense of Humor | Got to make me laugh | ✓ | | |
| Communication | Fights fair, doesn't get too angry | ✓ | | |
| Listening Skills | Can listen to me after a bad day | | ✓ | |
| Sexual Chemistry | Knows his way around a bedroom | | ✓ | |
| Family Closeness | No mama's boys please | | ✓ | |
| Desire for Kids | Let's worry about that later | | | ✓ |
| Other | | | | |
| **Total Checks** | | 8 | 10 | 4 |

Now it's your turn. If you haven't filled in the chart yet, take a few minutes and provide your answers. Feel free to add your own additional qualities to round out the samples. Remember, we're not striving for perfection. So if your chart has too many must-haves, you need to ask yourself whether you're being realistic. On the flip side, if your chart is full of who-cares responses, are you really putting your all into this, and thinking of what's best for you? That's the point of adding up your score, to make sure you're not swinging too far in either direction. We're looking for a balanced scorecard here.

Let's talk offline for a minute: just because I'm suggesting you recognize some "who-cares" traits, it does not, under any circumstances mean you should cheat yourself and settle! It's simply a reminder that, in love, as in business, you need to know when to pick your battles. Do you remember when we talked earlier about negotiating a deal? You obviously would prefer to have all of your terms met, and to walk away from the agreement with everything you wanted signed, sealed, and delivered. Because this rarely happens, you need to understand what is a deal breaker for you, and what is simply a little icing on the cake before heading into a relationship. Would you really let that perfect client walk out the door over a minor detail? Would you walk away even if you successfully negotiated all the big stuff?

At the same time, definitely remember that you're a go-getter at work, you've got your act together, and you deserve someone special. So, don't undersell yourself! Go for it and reach for that person who would be worthy of your love.

## It's Soul Statement Time

Can you see this great guy coming to life? Do you feel like you already know him? Can you almost reach out and touch him? I hope the answers are yes, yes, yes! That's what the Wishin' Statement and must-have, nice-to-have, who-cares exercises are all about. You have taken the abstract concept of meeting a great guy and brought him to life. Very few people ever take the time to do this, so congratulate yourself. If we were at work right now, it would clearly be reward and recognition time. You'd get another shiny plaque to proudly display on your wall, this time declaring, "I know exactly what I'm looking for out there!"

Now that this picture is crystallized in your mind and on paper, it's time to write some clear goals to make it happen. A vision without goals is like a ship with no destination. So let's put a rudder on your ship and find some direction.

### Women's Intuition

Wondering what a goal-oriented mindset at work can do for you in relationships? Check out Melinda's take on goal setting. She's forty-one and divorced, with a teenage daughter at home:

"The most successful women are the ones with the most drive. They have a goal, they work to achieve that goal, and they do not allow distractions to disrupt their progress. These are great qualities at work, and they can be applied to bring a fabulous guy into your life. I got this wrong the first time around with my ex-husband, but I know I'll get it right the second time around."

## Goals and Sub-Goals and Love—Oh My!

I'm going to go out on a limb here and assume that your overriding goal is to meet a great guy. If that's not your top goal, then can I interest you in a book outside the dating and relationship section at your local bookstore?

"I want to find a great guy" is the right top-line goal to have, but it's still too vague to just make happen. That's what sub-goals are for. They take that sometimes overwhelming top-line goal and break it down into more manageable, actionable sub-goals. The idea is that each of the sub-goals feels small enough to go after without being overwhelmed. You add up enough small goal accomplishments, and pretty soon you've reached your main goal, that great guy.

So what are the sub-goals that might go with the main goal of meeting that great guy? Here are five sub-goal examples to get your innovative, resourceful juices flowing:

1.  Break up with my current boyfriend, who I know is not a great guy.
2.  Join an online dating service to meet lots of new prospects.

3. Cut down on the late hours and weekends at work to free up time for more dates.
4. Give more solid guys second and third dates to stop canceling them out so quick.
5. Ask out that cute guy at the gym who I've had a crush on for two years.

## Corporate Memo

TO: All Employees
FROM: Carol Cohen
RE: Your Love Life

Goals and sub-goals are really common at work, especially when we set our plans and strategies at the beginning of the year or even start a new project later in the year. Many of our goals start off as vague, top-line goals. They can seem overwhelming and undefined at first. Then we start breaking down those goals into sub-goals, and pretty soon that nervous feeling fades away. It's replaced by our hardworking, go-getter attitude and we start seeing a crystal-clear road to the finish line.

Goal writing in dating and relationships is the exact same thing. I spent many a night sipping cosmopolitan martinis with my girlfriends and colleagues at work, talking and talking about meeting that spectacular guy. Once we move from pining over why he has not just appeared and breaking down that vague notion into sub-goals for how to find him, we start to see a path to success that isn't so painful or scary. As that path becomes more and more clear, it's inspiring! Hey, we can be self-starters and achieve success on our corporate projects, and we can definitely apply that same logic and triumph to our big love project!

Jeff gave you five examples of sub-goals to jumpstart your imagination and bolster creative thinking. But I'll bet you can come up with your own sub-goals by simply applying those very same goal-setting principles you use so often at work.

## I've Shown You Mine, Now You Show Me Yours

You get the idea here. You've got to break down that main goal into sub-goals. Otherwise you might never get off the ground. So let's start right here by writing your main goal. If you want to use my example of finding a great guy, that's great. If that's not your exact goal, then that's okay too. Put the pen to paper right here, right now, and let's bring your goal to life.

My top dating goal is to: _____

_____

_____

There it is in plain ink. Grab a sticky note and flag this page. Whenever you need some encouragement or feel lost along your dating journey, come back to this dating goal. *This* is why you're putting in the effort in the first place. Now, let's get more specific. I want you to write five specific sub-goals that you know would get you closer to your main goal. You can refer back to my sub-goal examples or brainstorm your own. Just make sure that each sub-goal would help you work toward making your main goal a reality. Be as specific as possible so your personal marching orders are clear and easy to implement. As always, you can complete the list here or in the back of the book as part of your Dating Business Plan.

Sub-goal #1 _____

_____

Sub-goal #2 _____

_____

Sub-goal #3 _____

_____

Sub-goal #4 _____

_____

Sub-goal #5 _____

_____

## You Need That By When?

If you've ever held a job of any kind, you know deadlines are a part of every business. When your boss says, "I need this by five o'clock," you get it done. While it's true that deadlines cause pressure and a sense of urgency, they also give us a timeframe to get something done. I know many of us believe in self-motivation. But let's be honest, there's something about expecting something by a certain time that gives us that kick in the pants to make it happen.

### action item

⟨If you can set timelines and milestones at work, why can't you do the same in dating and relationships? I've seen so many single women cruise through their projects, making deadline after deadline. Yet somehow this process breaks down in the dating world. Somehow, when it comes to dating, I hear things like "If it's meant to be, he'll come into my life." You'd never make a comment like that at work. Imagine telling your boss, "If this project is meant to be, it will just get done." That thinking wouldn't fly at work, so why hold yourself to a lower standard in dating? Instead, let's focus on really taking charge of our dating destinies. Don't rely on fate to find your mate. Make the action come to you!⟩

### *There's No Time Like the Present*

You've done a great job writing out your top-line dating goal and five sub-goals that support your overall goal. Now let's put a timeframe on these accomplishments and set some milestones to make sure you're on track with your dating game plan.

To help you along, let's revisit one of the sample sub-goals. On our sample list, sub-goal #2 was to join an online dating service to meet lots of new prospects. Let's bring that sub-goal to life, first by establishing a deadline to get it done. How about we say you have two weeks to sign up for your first online dating service. We know we've got fourteen days to make it happen. Now let's put some milestones alongside your deadline to stay on track. Here are three specific, tangible, and action-oriented milestones you could add to the sub-goal of joining an online dating service:

1.  Ask friends and family for recommendations on good online dating services.

2. Take a free test drive of the top two or three recommended online dating sites to find the right one for me.

3. Submit my photo and complete an online profile to get up and running with the chosen site.

It's up to you whether you need to break down the fourteen days into smaller time chunks. This really depends on how much discipline you feel you need to get the job done. The more specific you can be, the better your odds of getting it done on time. Whatever you do, don't let excuses get in the way. For example, let's say you're afraid to give online dating a shot for safety concerns. Protect your personal phone number at *www.aliasonline.com*.

---

## Corporate Memo

TO: All Employees
FROM: Carol Cohen
RE: Your Love Life

---

I can't tell you how many times a project at work has seemed daunting at first. It's like this new assignment has been dumped on your desk and your mind starts swirling with the deliverable. But then something happens in that smart, savvy mind of yours and you start to apply your past experiences to the current project. As businesswomen, we start breaking the goal down into smaller, simpler steps that don't scare us and help get us to the finish line.

Now apply this same business strategy to joining an online dating service. I have many friends, family members, and colleagues who, for one reason or another, can't seem to muster the will to join one. They have many reasons, from being overwhelmed at the number of sites to being stricken with a paralyzing fear of the unknown to being clueless about even getting the online dating process started. But look at Jeff's milestone breakdown. Does asking friends and family for recommendations seem overwhelming as a standalone task? Not really. The same goes for the other two milestones of test-driving a site or submitting a photo and profile. Just like breaking down that new project at work, if you string together enough dating milestones, pretty soon you'll have a life milestone on your hands—you'll have achieved your dating goal, and found "the One."

---

### Draw a Line in the Sand

Now it's time to revisit those five sub-goals you just wrote. For each sub-goal, I want you to first give yourself a deadline. Let's be honest, we all know what a temptation and flat-out obstacle procrastination can be in reaching your ultimate goals, so let's try to tackle that monster head-on by giving ourselves a target timeframe. Once you have a due date down on paper, I want you to also write two or three milestones that would help keep you on a fast track to success. You can do this right here or in your Dating Business Plan in the back of the book:

I will achieve sub-goal #1 by: _____

Here are three milestones that will keep me on track for sub-goal #1:

1. _____

_____

2. _____

_____

3. _____

_____

I will achieve sub-goal #2 by: _____

Here are three milestones that will keep me on track for sub-goal #2:

1. _____

_____

2. _____

_____

3. _____

_____

I will achieve sub-goal #3 by: _____
Here are three milestones that will keep me on track for sub-goal #3:

1. _____

   _____

2. _____

   _____

3. _____

   _____


I will achieve sub-goal #4 by: _____
Here are three milestones that will keep me on track for sub-goal #4:

1. _____

   _____

2. _____

   _____

3. _____

   _____


I will achieve sub-goal #5 by: _____
Here are three milestones that will keep me on track for sub-goal #5:

1. _____

   _____

2. _____

   _____

3. _____

   _____

# Metrics

What's the first thing your boss always asks you after delegating a new assignment or project? "How will we know we've been successful?" That's what success metrics are all about. They're quantitative and qualitative measures that help you measure whether your goals are having an impact. Quantitative metrics can be measured in financial or number-oriented terms. Qualitative metrics are more touchy-feely, say customer feedback or an employee survey. The two types of metrics combine together to give you a sense of whether or not your goals have accomplished what they set out to do.

---

## Corporate Memo

TO: All Employees
FROM: Carol Cohen
RE: Your Love Life

I should mention that my first job at American Express was director of strategic planning and measurement. Let's just say I took a real deep dive in understanding how metrics are the driving force behind achieving goals and objectives. It's the metrics and measurements that ultimately tell you whether you're on track or completely missing your goals. They are an objective and honest way of charting your progress. I think sometimes as businesswomen we know the importance of metrics at work, but we forget how they can help us in dating, too. There's no reason to just drift from date to date when we can have targets in the back of our mind to really crystallize our thinking about how each person gets us closer to or further from our ultimate dating destinies. That's why metrics can really tell you whether you gave it your all in your performance on the job front, or in this case, dating front!

---

When it comes to dating, metrics can offer a way to measure whether or not your goals, sub-goals, and milestones are on track. Let's look back at that sub-goal to join an online dating service. Are there some metrics we can brainstorm? Let's start with the quantitative.

## Quantitative Online Dating Service Metrics

1. Number of potential online dating sites considered and ultimately joined
2. Proof of online dating service membership (such as a credit card statement)
3. Activation notice from online dating service after a profile is completed and a photo is submitted

Do you get the idea here? All three of these quantitative metrics can be measured and proven as true or false. You can definitely count how many online sites you considered. Either the charge to join a site is on your credit card statement, or you didn't pay. Finally, the online site will most definitely forward a confirmation notice when you are officially up and running on the site.

Creating these specific, ambitious targets for yourself will not only keep your focused, go-getter attitude on track, it will also help you avoid giving up too easily after one site might not have worked out for you. It can be all too easy to just give up after only a couple of tries, but we all know that would never fly on the job scene, and there should be no excuse for giving up on something even more important on the dating scene!

### Women's Intuition

Metrics don't have to be complicated; you can make them simple and straightforward. Here's Tracy's idea of a dating metric. She's an advertising executive in Dallas:

"If I had to set a metric on dating, it would be the total number of fun dates in a given time period. This way, it doesn't depend on the number of men or total number of dates. Instead, it's just about having fun!"

### Qualitative Online Dating Service Metrics

1. Feedback from friends, family, or online reviews from people who have used each online site
2. Friendliness and knowledge of online customer service staff that helps sign you up for a site
3. Ease of site use in creating your profile or submitting the photo

Unlike the quantitative metrics, these three qualitative success measures cannot be summed up with a yes-or-no answer. Still, they're equally important to the quantitative metrics.

## Welcome to the Metric System

Now it's your turn. Go back to your five sub-goals and think of some metrics, either quantitative or qualitative, that will help you know if your sub-goals are on track. Go to your Dating Business Plan in Appendix 1 or fill it out right here:

Three quantitative or qualitative metrics that will help me measure my success for sub-goal #1 are:

**1.** _____

_____

**2.** _____

_____

**3.** _____

_____

Three quantitative or qualitative metrics that will help me measure my success for sub-goal #2 are:

**1.** _____

_____

**2.** _____

_____

**3.** _____

_____

Three quantitative or qualitative metrics that will help me measure my success for sub-goal #3 are:

1. _____

_____

2. _____

_____

3. _____

_____


Three quantitative or qualitative metrics that will help me measure my success for sub-goal #4 are:

1. _____

_____

2. _____

_____

3. _____

_____


Three quantitative or qualitative metrics that will help me measure my success for sub-goal #5 are:

1. _____

_____

2. _____

_____

3. _____

_____

## All Aboard for Your Reward

Hey, I know it's not easy to break down this whole dating thing. That's especially true if you've never realized the wisdom and power already within you to approach dating from a logical, business-minded approach. Let me be the first to congratulate you for applying your business skills to writing quality dating goals, sub-goals to back them up, and milestones and metrics to track and measure your success. You are officially off and running toward meeting that exceptional person worthy of your affection!

We've got one final business principle, research and development, to cover in this section. In *Dating, Inc.* we call this Research and Envelopment because you need to wrap yourself up in this chapter. I know, I know, right now you're probably feeling that bright spark, that chomping-at-the-bit, ready-to-go-after-those-goals feeling. As much as I want you to jump right into accomplishing your goals, it's important to have some fun and research what's been successfully done by others before you, as well as what's worked versus not worked in your past dating approach. No need to reinvent the wheel here. You're not the first woman who's ever dated, and by taking the time for Research and Envelopment, you can re-evaluate both your dating past and the dating past of other remarkably smart women like you. We've all had some dating successes along with some dating mistakes or blunders. No matter how big or small those blunders were, it's okay that they happened. The point is not to be hard on yourself for your dating past, but rather to be smart about your dating future. Use your sensible wisdom and skill to avoid what has not worked and learn from what worked like a charm! It will also get you to your goal faster because you'll learn the best practices out there from other savvy, single businesswomen just like you.

## The Bottom Line

You're ready to move on to the next chapter if the following statements are all true:

- You understand the difference between Goals and Objectives and Souls and Objectives.

- You completed your chart covering must-have, nice-to-have, and who-cares qualities.
- You turned your chart into a top-line dating goal and sub-goals associated with achieving your main goal.
- You created deadlines, milestones, and metrics to make sure you are on track and will be successful.

# chapter
# **three**

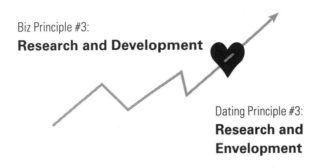

Biz Principle #3:
**Research and Development**

Dating Principle #3:
**Research and Envelopment**

## Agenda

- The role of research and development in organizations
- How research and development in business translates into Research and Envelopment in dating
- Why Envelopment begins with the honesty phase
- How to benchmark or compare your dating strategies against other successful singles on the market
- Best practices in dating, how to learn those strategies, and how to add them to your dating repertoire

## Work/Life Balance

Do you ever have one of those mornings where you just need that extra cup of coffee or tea? You've been bouncing from meeting to meeting and call to call, yet it's still only 10:30 A.M. Sometimes that extra burst of caffeine gives you just the kick you need to make it through the morning. So you decide to make a quick run to the local coffee shop.

The servers behind the counter know you well—you're a regular. Five minutes later you're back in the elevator, mocha latte #2 in hand.

Your thoughts swirl on the to-do's that lie ahead. Just as you're about to sit down, you notice a sticky note on your keyboard. It's from your colleague down the hall, and he needs some quick help with a riddle that's stumped him since yesterday. Looking at the sticky, you smile and wrap your hands around the warmth of the latte. You can see it's another word jumble giving you encouragement on the next step in your dating journey.

EB  OETSHN  HIWT  FEROLSUY  _____

As soon as you unscramble this morning's jumble, you'll have helped your colleague with an important message and decoded the key tip in this chapter. Research and development in business and in dating requires this slogan to be successful. As always, if you're stumped, see the back of this book for the answer key.

## Corporate Memo

TO: All Employees
FROM: Carol Cohen
RE: Your Love Life

Think about that word "honesty" for a moment. So much of our approach in business is based on it. When we do a self appraisal, we're honest about our performance so we can make it even stronger. When we deliver performance reviews to direct reports, we're honest about their performance to help them reflect on what's working well and what needs to improve. When we talk to suppliers, buyers, and customers, we're straight shooters to meet and exceed expectations and strengthen working relationships. In each of these situations, everyone can agree rationally that if we just ignore any performance issues, they will *not* just magically go away.

Somehow though, when it comes to dating and relationships, the emotional element kicks in. That honest, direct style that makes us successful at work vanishes, becomes a lot harder to voice, or downright frightens us. We lose that ability to be honest about the guys we're dating and what we want in relationships. But deep down, when we apply logical, business principles to our dating approach, that light bulb turns on and we know it doesn't have to be that way. If we can tell a direct report or supplier his or her strengths and development areas, then certainly we can muster the courage to look at the good and bad in our own dating approach. We have the power, savvy, and skill to think emotionally and rationally. We can consciously decide that we won't just ignore our performance issues. We won't simply ignore what's preventing us from reaching our dating goals. We will do this because we know from our business approach that if we don't course-correct our faults and strengthen our dating tactics, we're not using our full arsenal of skills. We know intuitively, in business and in dating, that if we're not honest with ourselves, our performance issues will not just magically go away. So, let's grab these learnings by the horns, and learn from our best practices, shall we?

## It's R & D Time!
## (That's Research and Development)

> From: your.boss@work.com
> To: you@work.com
> Subject: Research
> I'm off to a meting. B4 we launch dis new product, we need to research da best practices out theere and learn frum dem.
> Tanks for making it happen.

When a company wants to launch a new product or service, they don't go into the process blindly. The company wants to know what's already in the marketplace, what the best practices are, and what their current or potential customers think about the idea. The main goal in this business approach is to be a winner in the marketplace. The company wants their product or service to be desirable and attract the best potential customers.

That's the essence of this e-mail from your boss. It's basically like your boss is saying, "Look, I know you're a go-getter, and I have no doubt you'll create a great product. But before you jump into action, let's do our homework. Check the competition, research the best practices, and let's put ourselves in the best possible position to be successful."

Let's talk offline for a minute: when you tell people about the great new book you're reading that teaches you to apply business principles to dating, undoubtedly some of them will say, "Business and dating? Those topics just don't mix!" As we've discussed, these naysayers and doubters base that belief on the fact that business is about logic, and dating is about love and emotions. By now I'm sure we all agree that that perspective is too narrow, and misses out on the power of both to maximize your success. I want to bring up this point again now because I've just introduced the key business concepts of competitive analysis, benchmarking, and best practices. These three terms are definitely logic based, but now we've seen how they can tie into an emotional decision. When you combine both logic and emotion, you get the best of both worlds. That's what I'm talking about when I say apply business concepts to your dating life.

## A Quick Business Explanation of Research and Development

Let's start basic, with the definition of research and development from a business perspective. We'll break the concept down together and then easily apply it to dating.

> **JEFF'S DEF•I•NI•TIONS:** According to InvestorWords.com, research and development is the process of discovering new knowledge about products, processes, and services, and then applying that knowledge to create new and improved products, processes, and services that fill market needs.

### Say What?

Let me break that definition down for you because it offers powerful business lessons in our approach to dating. Basically, research is all about gathering existing knowledge, and development is all about applying that knowledge. So if you only remember two words from this definition, make sure those words are "gathering" and "applying." That's what research and development are all about.

### Research and Development at Work

So how might an organization break down the R & D phase? For the purposes of this book, we're going to assume this is not a highly technical R & D project, say for a new computer or satellite. Let's keep it simple. It will get us to the dating side of the story quicker! In simplest terms, we can break down research and development into five key steps:

1. **The current state:** every R & D project needs to start with an assessment of the current state of affairs. What's good, bad, and needs improving about the company right now? What's not working in their approach that can be improved?

2. **Feedback:** Beyond a company doing its own self-review, it's important to also ask for feedback from the people who know the company best. This might include customers, suppliers, buyers, and employees—anyone who interacts with the company and can provide some insights and perspective.

3. **Competitive analysis:** What else is out there? What are the competitors already offering? How will the company offering be similar or different?

4. **Best practices:** Are there any best practices in the marketplace that the company should learn from and even include in its own offering?

5. **Implementation:** How can the company take everything it has learned and package it up into the final product or service offering?

## Corporate Memo

TO: All Employees
FROM: Carol Cohen
RE: Your Love Life

I really believe in research and development. I know that as go-getter, successful women, we're into action and results. There's nothing like finishing an assignment, winning new business, or closing a sale. However, there are times when slowing down to research the industry, check the best practices, and ask for feedback can really help speed up your success in the long run. Taking this valuable time can make a "good" product or service become "great". It can also make a *good* dater a *great* dater!

---

### *Research and Development in Action*

Let's walk through one example of these five steps just to make sure it's clear. By the time we're done, you'll be so eager to jump right to how we apply it to dating. But first, we've got to make sure the business concepts are clear.

Let's pretend we own a juice-making company together. We currently offer only orange juice, but we're thinking of expanding into grape juice. How might we work through the five steps?

1. **The current state:** First, we're currently in the orange-juice business, not the grape-juice business. So we need to accept that we're entering new territory. We'd want to examine whether we've ever tried to expand into new juice flavors before. If so, what went well, and what might have caused failure?

2. **Feedback:** We would definitely go out to our loyal orange-juice customers as well as prospective grape-juice customers for feedback. We'd want to know what they like about our product, what they think could be better, and what's important to them in choosing a grape juice.

3. **Competitive analysis:** Who else already makes grape juice? What makes them successful? How will our product compare to their product?

4. **Best practices:** What industry practices from grape-juice makers should we emulate? Before we start making grape juice from scratch, could we simply mix in some of these best practices to make the best possible product?

5. **Implementation:** Now that we have all this great juice research, how can we put it all together to make a great product?

## Less Juice, More Dating

Okay, all this juice talk is making me thirsty. Let's switch over to the dating scene and see how research and development in business translates into Research and Envelopment in dating and relationships. We start with a new e-mail just in from your boss:

> From: your.boss@work.com
> To: you@work.com
> Subject: Envelopment
> I'm off to a meting. B4 you meet a grate partner, we need to research da best dating practices out theere and learn frum dem.
> Tanks for making it happen.

Your boss is still interested in research and development, but this time, we're not launching a new product—we're finding a great partner. So let's start with the definition of Research and Envelopment, then we'll apply the five steps to dating.

**JEFF'S DEF•I•NI•TIONS:** According to *Dating, Inc.*, Research and Envelopment is the process of discovering new dating and relationship knowledge and then applying that knowledge to create new and improved dating tactics.

### Women's Intuition

Before we break down Research and Envelopment, listen to Sara, a technology consultant in Sydney, Australia, who sent in a great way to think about applying this topic based on how she approaches software initiatives. By the way, Sara landed a really great guy of her own. Could the software design lifecycle have played a role?

"The software design lifecycle includes four key steps, and these really do apply to dating, too:

1.  **Design:** We spend time thinking about the product and meeting with our client to design the best software application—one that will meet our client's needs. In the dating world, this should be time well spent thinking about what qualities you want in a partner and going on various dates to determine what qualities are important to you in a partner.

2.  **Testing:** We test our software before delivering it to the client (we run through different "real life" scenarios using the application) . . . relationships are also tested out for a period of time before they go into full swing.

3.  **Implementation:** We implement our software by training users on how to use the application, and do a bit of change management to make sure their transition is as smooth as possible. In the dating world, this is just like the first month or two of dating . . . it can be rocky because you're learning new things about the other person and teaching them about yourself.

4.  **After-care support:** After the software has been implemented, we provide after-care support in case the users have questions about how to use the application or they want some new features added to the software. This is like your network of friends in the dating world—they are there to listen to you complain about your relationship problems and provide you with advice on how to make the relationship work."

## Step 1: The Current State

Just like business, we're going to start with the current state. In *Dating, Inc.* we need to answer one very important question. Why are you so successful at work but can't seem to find the right guy in your relationship? I didn't want to just provide theory here, so I asked for three perspectives on this issue. I asked a single woman, a married woman, and a single guy. Here are their answers and theories on this question:

### The Single Woman's Perspective
Carrie, 27, Associate Editor from New York

"I know some women like this and have definitely asked myself this question! It could be that these women just don't know how to have fun. Without fun they have a lot of time on their hands to spend at work. They can't get a date because they're not leaving the office to go and have some fun. It could also be that these women may be too demanding or bossy to their partner, which scares the men away. I wonder too, if it's a self-fulfilling prophecy where a successful woman may tell herself she doesn't have time for relationships and may sabotage any hope of one."

### The Married Woman's Perspective
Melanie, 32, Fashion Consultant from Los Angeles

"I have a close girlfriend who is extraordinarily successful in her career, landing one promotion after the next, but has not had a serious boyfriend in over ten years. For the longest time, we all chalked it up to her boyfriend ten years ago doing a real number on her (they were living together, he was too chicken to break up with her, so he started bringing other women to the house until she kicked him out). Years later, she's still coming up with really lame excuses why she can't continue to see a guy: he wears bad shoes (her number one complaint), he's never been to Asia or Europe, he's not 'artsy' enough, he's not 'sexy' enough, he's not 'interesting' enough . . . the list goes on.

Now I've come to realize that she's just scared of getting hurt, so it's easier for her to have superficial, short-term relationships with men. Even though she says she wants to meet someone and have a meaningful relationship, her expectations of a potential partner are all wrong. I think women who have been successful in business should try to see relationships in the same way as getting another promotion or landing the next great account. You can't forget about continuing to work hard at the relationship. Just like a company wants employees who add to their success, men are still looking for a partner who complements them, not someone who is just like them or who wants to change them.

What amazes me most about falling in love with the man who became my husband is that he is still 'wowing' me with his kindness, his sense of humor, and his loyalty to friends and family. These are not things that you can learn about a person after a couple of dates. You have to go beyond all the superficial aspects—like his taste in shoes. Those bad shoes can even become endearing once you discover other good qualities about a person. I think women take for granted that finding a great guy and having a successful relationship takes time, energy, and doesn't just happen overnight. I wish they could see it takes the same amount of time and energy—if not more!—that led to their success at work in getting promoted or landing that big account."

### The Single Guy's Perspective
Chris, Third-Year Med School Student from Philadelphia

"I have a theory on this issue. I believe that it is all about focus . . . some women who are totally focused on their career don't leave room for a relationship to develop. It can be easier for men, because bachelorhood is more socially accepted and men can get hitched much later without having to worry about their ability to have a family."

## ···state of the business #3 ············
There are more than 18 million women in the U.S. labor force who have never been married, nearly 9 million divorced, and 2 million widowed. That totals 29 million savvy, single businesswomen out there who deserve a great guy and can now find one by applying business tactics to get bold results in love.

### What's Your Perspective?
Okay, you've heard the perspective of a single woman, a married woman, and a single guy. They all have their theories on why women are successful at work but not in relationships. Some of their comments may have seemed spot-on. Others may have infuriated you. You may have even gained a new insight. The reality is that only one perspective actually matters in this next exercise—yours!

So now it's honesty time. You need to assess the current state. You're a SuperStar at work, so what's the truth in your relationships? Take the time here to write down a few sentences describing the current state of your dating approach and results. If it's anything like the three perspectives we shared, by all means, borrow the thoughts and theories (as always, you can fill out this section or work in the back of the book). Basically, you're trying to answer one question as honestly as possible about yourself . . . why are you so successful at work but can't seem to find the right guy in your relationship?

_____

_____

_____

---

## Corporate Memo

**TO:** All Employees
**FROM:** Carol Cohen
**RE:** Your Love Life

---

We all have a friend who just refuses to be honest about her approach to dating. She has excuses for not dating or makes excuses for the below-par guys she does date. Meanwhile, you sit around wishing she could just get real with herself. You just want to reach out, grab her firmly, and break it down for her. But for some reason, she just won't change her patterns. Let's not make that same mistake in our own lives, as we read this book. If we were at work and something clearly wasn't working, we'd make a change. The same approach must hold true for you in dating. So take a minute and reread what you just wrote. Pretend I'm your good friend and we're sipping on hot tea in a cozy cafe, talking about dating and relationships. Would you be able to look me in the eye, read what you just wrote, and know that it truly describes the current state of your dating approach? If so, then you're on your way to meeting a great guy. If not, don't worry about it. Just go back, find that honest place, and rewrite your entry.

---

## Step 2: It's Feedback Time

Most of us like hearing positive feedback, but few of us like to hear criticism, no matter how constructive the comments. However, if you're going to make some dating changes, you need to hear both sides of the story. So here's where you'll hear the good, the bad, and the ugly about your dating approach. To get the best possible mix of feedback, you're going to listen to four sources:

1.  Yourself
2.  Close friends and family
3.  Ex-partners (if they'll still talk to you/you'll still talk to them)
4.  Your target guy

### It's Me Time!

Let's start with you. We've already covered the tough, ugly, hard-to-look-at side of things. Now let's turn positive. What qualities do you possess that make you a real catch? Need some help shedding that modesty? We asked a couple of women to share their absolutely best qualities, including most memorable compliments, and here's what we heard.

#### Meet Julie, a hard-working Business Consultant based in Singapore

"I'm the best person to be in a relationship with! Guys always have good things to say about me. I'm easy-going, funny, I get along with almost everyone, I'm thoughtful, and of course, kind to animals (even mice)."

#### Meet Alice, an outgoing Public Relations Executive based in Hartford, Connecticut

"I'm even-tempered, thoughtful, committed to making relationships successful, considerate, and always willing to put needs of others before mine."

#### Meet Devon, a laid-back Freelance Writer based in New Orleans, Louisiana

"They might say that I'm very loving and giving in a relationship. The other person is a priority to me and they can definitely feel it. I go out of my way with little signs of letting them know that they matter. It doesn't even have to cost a dime because it's more from the heart. An ex told me once that no one had ever loved him in the way that I had and he genuinely feared no one ever would again."

### Now Toot Your Own Horn

You get the idea here. You had to answer the tough questions about your lack of success in the previous section; now let's hear the good stuff. Are you like Julie, Alice, and Devon, or are you great in your own way?

Come on, I know you can describe your strengths in the office, so let's hear about your dating and relationship strengths. In the space provided, write down a brief paragraph describing exactly what makes you great to date. You know what? Don't worry about making it brief—go nuts! This is about what makes you absolutely unique and desirable to date, so let the self-compliments roll. (You know the drill by now—you can do this here or as part of your Dating Business Plan in the back. How about we make an agreement going forward that I won't write this reminder anymore? I'm sure by now you have your own system going anyway):

_____

_____

_____

### Women's Intuition

Deirdre is a single waitress in San Diego, California, and actively dating. She offers another great way to look at dating strengths and opportunities, for you and those great guys you'll soon be meeting:

*"Do your own internal quarterly review every three months or so to make sure you are headed down the right track in the love department. At each evaluation, ask yourself some important questions. Is this person still a good fit for me? Are we still having fun and getting along well? Has our communication gotten better, worse, or stayed the same? Have we made any kind of progress in general since my last evaluation? If things are looking good and you're still into it, be honest and make recommendations for areas of improvement for both you and your partner."*

### My Mom Says This, My Best Friend Says That

We've got your perspective on the table, now what about your friends and family? If you have the time and want to hear it directly from them, go ahead and ask. It could make for a fun and bonding conversation. But if you prefer not to ask, I'll bet you already know the answer. Think back to Thanksgiving dinner last year. What did your mom and dad, your brother, or Uncle Earl say about the state of your singlehood? Now think about the last time you went for coffee with your best friend. I'll bet you spent part of the time talking guys. What advice did she give you? What did she say you should do differently?

Now put the top three to five very specific feedback themes and highlights all together into your dating strengths and opportunities (we prefer to avoid the word *weaknesses,* it's too negative for a book about taking charge of your love life) as perceived by your close friends and family.

**Top Three to Five Dating Strengths:**

1. _____

_____

2. _____

_____

3. _____

_____

4. _____

_____

5. _____

_____

**Top Three to Five Dating Opportunities:**

1. _____

_____

2. _____

_____

3. _____

_____

4. _____

_____

5. _____

_____

### What Would My Ex Say?

I know the answer to this question: "Who cares!" Now, I'm not suggesting you have to call up your ex-boyfriend, especially if you haven't spoken to him since you walked out on his sorry you know what. But I am asking you to think from his perspective. I'll bet he said some great things about you at the beginning of the relationship and some not-so-great things toward the end.

Without stirring up the emotions from the breakup, what did your last boyfriend (or better yet, last few boyfriends) say made you easy and not so easy to date? What would they say are your top dating strengths and dating opportunities?

**Top Three to Five Dating Strengths:**

1. _____

_____

2. _____

_____

3. _____

_____

4. _____

_____

5. _____

_____

**Top Three to Five Dating Opportunities:**

1. _____

_____

2. _____

_____

3. _____

_____

**4.** _____

_____

**5.** _____

_____

---

## Corporate Memo

TO: All Employees
FROM: Carol Cohen
RE: Your Love Life

---

When Jeff first told me about asking, or just pretending to ask, your ex-boyfriend for relationship feedback, I thought he was crazy! Who wants to stir up all those emotions or relive something that didn't work out? It's so much easier to just move forward and never speak of the failed relationship again.

Then I started thinking from a logical business perspective again. I realized that ex-boyfriends are a lot like failed business ventures, dissatisfied customers, and unsuccessful product launches. They're painful to accept, but deep down we know there's a ton of learning to be done there. So if we can learn from our mistakes at work to create stronger business ventures, there's absolutely no reason we can't think back to our exes and revisit what went well versus what could have been better to create stronger dating ventures.

---

### *Back to the Future with Your Target Guy*

If you found it difficult to stir up the good and bad from your last relationship, then you might be confused by asking for feedback from a guy you haven't even met yet.

**action item**

Even though you've never met your target guy (or maybe you have, but you're not dating yet), by now you have a great visual of him. Think back to the first two chapters, specifically your Wishin' Statement and must-have, nice-to-have, who-cares qualities. We ended up painting a truly vivid picture of your target guy. So before you say, "How can I get feedback from a guy I never met?" realize that you have met this guy in your mind and on paper right here in this book. Here's a guy you have described so clearly, I'll bet you actually could answer on his behalf. Just think about what he'd say after your first few dates. What about you would leave him begging for more? What would he tell his friends he didn't like about you? Why would he be interested or not so interested in another date with you?〉

Keep that bright idea in mind and really try to see that target guy. Pretend you just went on that first date. He's home now, talking to his buddy about the date. His buddy says, "How did it go, do you like her?" Your target guys says, "We had a great time, I can already see things I love about her, and a few things I wish I could change." Put yourself in that conversation and write down what your target guy would likely say about your top three to five dating strengths and opportunities:

**Top Three to Five Dating Strengths:**

1. _____

_____

2. _____

_____

3. _____

_____

4. _____

_____

5. _____

_____

**Top Three to Five Dating Opportunities:**

1. _____

_____

2. _____

_____

3. _____

_____

**4.** _____

_____

**5.** _____

_____

## Feedback Themes

Now it's time to put it all together. You've written down your thoughts, plus the thoughts of your friends and family, ex-partner, and target guy. As with any feedback, some of it is more valuable, some of it less so. The key is to look for themes. If two or more people had similar comments, then it's probably true. If only one person mentioned something, good or bad, then definitely ask yourself about the validity of that particular comment.

## One Woman's Rollup

Meet Loretta. She's a lawyer at an entertainment law firm in Los Angeles, California. She's had three serious boyfriends in the fourteen years since college. At age thirty-four, she's ready to meet the "One." After checking with herself, her best friend Sheila, her sister and father, two exes that she's still friends with, and visualizing her ideal guy, here's what she came up with:

### Loretta's Great Qualities/Improvement Areas Chart

| Person Giving Feedback | Great Qualities | Improvement Areas |
|---|---|---|
| Your Thoughts | Sense of humor, Giving and patient | Talk too much, Out of shape |
| Friends & Family | Great smile, Very giving | Disorganized, Don't smile enough |
| Ex-Partners | Spontaneous, Great in bed | Not a good dresser, Talk too much |
| Target Person | Great smile, Inviting eyes | Out of shape, Not a good dresser |

Loretta saw themes in the great qualities and improvement areas right away after completing this exercise. As you can see, some qualities are listed multiple times, and other qualities only make Loretta's list once. For example, everyone agrees that Loretta has a great smile and is very giving. On the flip side, Loretta seems to be out of shape and could use a wardrobe overhaul. Also notice that one of her greatest strengths, the smile, came up as an opportunity area. "It was interesting to hear that my family doesn't think I smile enough. In essence, it made me realize that I'm totally wasting a dating strength by underutilizing it!"

### Rollup #2

Meet Peggy. She's a chiropractor based in Jacksonville, Florida. She's had a string of two- to three-month relationships in the last eight years. Peggy is not thinking marriage just yet, but she would like to meet a guy who is not afraid of commitment and won't run at the first sign of trouble. After thinking about herself, asking her sister and aunt for feedback, checking with her last semi-serious boyfriend, and visualizing her dream guy, here's what she came up with:

**Peggy's Great Qualities/Improvement Areas Chart**

| Person Giving Feedback | Great Qualities | Improvement Areas |
|---|---|---|
| **Your Thoughts** | Funny, Good listener, Thoughtful, Creative | Patience in all areas, Too trusting |
| **Friends & Family** | Gentle, Easy to talk to, Pretty, Beautiful, Very loving, Honest | Puts everyone else first, Messy apartment, Sometimes act too quick |
| **Ex-Partners** | Supportive, Open mind, Beautiful, Loving, Honest, Creative | Letting go of past hurts, Patience |
| **Target Person** | Thoughtful, Kind, giving, Good listener, eyes | Follow instincts more, Messy apartment |

What do we see as themes in Peggy's chart? "I realized that clearly I'm a great listener, a very warm and loving person, and I have a giving, gentle spirit. It felt good to realize that many people I know and love (or loved) share these ideas about me." On the opportunity side, it looks like Peggy needs to clean her apartment and maybe pull back from being so trusting and giving. "On the flip side of things, it was eye-opening to realize that so many people think I'm *too* nice. I've always thought to myself, I should really work on that—now I think I really will!" You get the idea here. By looking at the consolidated results from all the people who know you best, you can identify the dating strengths and opportunities that matter most.

### Your Rollup

You have the feedback from those who know you best, and you've seen Loretta and Peggy's examples. Now it's your turn again. What are the themes that came up, both the good and bad, from the different people polled? Fill in your own chart on the following page now.

**Your Great Qualities/Improvement Areas Chart**

| Person Giving Feedback | Great Qualities | Improvement Areas |
|---|---|---|
| Your Thoughts | | |
| Friends & Family | | |
| Ex-Partners | | |
| Target Person | | |

## Step 3: Who Just Caught the Eye of Your Target Guy?

In the business world, I'll bet you are familiar with competitive analysis and benchmarking. That is where you check out what your rivals have to offer. You figure out what's unique about your product offering to encourage potential customers to select you, not your competitors.

So, what's unique about you? We've just spent some serious time reviewing your dating strengths, so these things should be fresh in your mind. We've also brought to life your ideal guy by writing your Wishin' Statement and must-have, nice-to-have, and who-cares write-ups. You now know in your heart that you want and deserve this great guy, and you have a very keen sense of what you'll have to offer him going into the relationship. However, this great guy has choices out there (especially if he's as great as you've described), same as you. Of course, once he meets fabulous you, he will choose you over any of those other potential mates. Nevertheless, by looking at other available women out there, particularly ones who might be interested in the same guys as you, you can pick up some tips and ideas from their approach to dating that will only make your approach more effective. After all, our goal is to make sure *you* catch the eye of your target guy.

---

## Corporate Memo

TO: All Employees
FROM: Carol Cohen
RE: Your Love Life

---

In business we fully understand the threat of competitors. We know they can steal our ideas, woo our customers, and potentially run us out of business. But we can also learn from our competitors. Sometimes we see a particular sales approach or product style and it gives us an idea to improve our own product or service offering. Eventually all of the competitors feed off each other and raise their games. In the end, this competition drives the best possible offerings for the end consumers.

Now, let's think about what we can learn from other women using a similar angle. I'm sure you can remember a time where you were in a café or at a party and saw something intriguing about another single woman. Maybe it was the way she wore her hair, a trendy outfit, how she carried herself. You thought to yourself that you'd love to emulate that particular trait.

You can consider those thoughts competitive analysis applied to dating. No, we're not talking about fighting over men, here. We're too confident and too successful in our lives to do that. But we can learn from other women out there. We can see what's working and add it to our dating repertoire.

---

### *Analysis Paralysis*

So get out there and see what's really working. Sit in a bar, coffeeshop, or bookstore one day and observe. Watch what the single women are doing. What can you emulate? What should you avoid? Or ask your single friends who you believe are great daters. What do they do that really works on the singles scene? What are some pitfalls and traps to avoid? Really dive into this research. The more ideas you can glean from analyzing the others, the more positive tweaks you can make to your own dating style. Remember, it's all about enjoying the ride. So have some fun along the way, and see what your fellow singles are up to on the singles scene.

Let's talk offline for a minute: look, this is not a dating overhaul. I'm not suggesting you trash your wardrobe, change your hairstyle, join the gym, revamp your personality, or become something that you are not. By all means, do *not* do all of that! You will attract the wrong guy and make yourself miserable trying to be something that you're not! What I am saying, though, is that minor modifications in your style or approach can add up to big dating advantages. Do you remember that feedback section earlier on Loretta? Her great smile is one of her top qualities, but her friends and family said she doesn't smile enough. So, show us those pearly whites, Loretta! And there you have it, an itty bitty dating tweak that could go a long way.

## Step 4: Practice Makes Perfect

Intrinsically related to the concept of competitive analysis is the idea of understanding best practices. Best practices are the absolute best ideas, concepts, and strategies to tackle a situation. Companies think about the big ones in their chosen industry, competitors who have stood the test of time, or made a serious impact on the marketplace, and identify the nuts-and-bolts tactics that made them so. There's no reason you can't use this great business strategy in dating too. So, get out there and start asking people for dating advice. What worked well for them and how did they land their Mr. Right? What advice would they offer someone trying to meet that special someone? I wanted to give you a head start on this, so I asked my network of friends and colleagues for the absolute best and worst dating advice they ever heard.

Here's a quick compilation of their thoughts, wisdom, and overall best practices.

### The Best Advice They Listened To
Boy, was I glad I listened when someone told me . . .

- "'Trust your gut!' Again and again I find this to be true! You can overlook that you like opera and he doesn't, or that he's a night owl and you love the mornings, but you know without analyzing the balance sheet if it truly has good chances of working out—your intuition is telling you."—Maria, 29, sales rep from Toledo, OH
- "'You have to find a middle ground when it comes to relationships.' I might not like to shop or watch chick flicks, but I'll do it for the right person. That means they have to sacrifice for me too!"—Will, 31, engineer from Phoenix, AZ
- "'You have to be able to juggle work, family, friends as well as relationships.' Making quality time for all is very important."—Tara, 33, project manager from Wilmington, DE
- "'Communication is critical.' Don't tell me you're not mad when you really are mad. Don't tell me you don't play games when you really do play a game. It's the 'no-game' game, and it ain't cool."—Jessica, 29, customer service rep from Orange County, CA
- "You can't force the love. If you're not feeling it, get out. The person could be the best-looking boyfriend or girlfriend you've ever dated, but if it's just not a fit, then get out."—Michael, 28, bartender from Boston, MA

### The Worst Advice and Why They Didn't Listen
Can you believe that someone once tried to tell me . . .

- "'You'll learn to like him and a sense of humor isn't all that important.' What*ever*—if the spark's not there from the beginning and you're never laughing, then the relationship is headed nowhere fast."—Elisa, 29, restaurant manager, Montreal
- "'Fighting is a sign of a healthy relationship.' Boy, were they wrong. I've come to realize that arguing is okay here and

there, but if it turns into constant fighting, with no positive outcomes, no improvements in your communication, then the relationship is anything but healthy."—John, 43, veterinarian from Orlando

- "'Blind dating is for losers.' I don't know why it has this negative perception. It's all about just meeting the right guy. How we meet is irrelevant. All that matters is that we meet somehow, some way."—Lizzie, 30, nanny from Chicago

- "'It's always all his fault.' It used to be so easy for me to blame guy after guy for a failed relationship. Finally, at some point, after hearing the same complaints from ex after ex, I realized that it takes two to tango, that I am also responsible for a relationship ending. It's not always about him (although it certainly is easier to believe that)."—Camilla, 28, art dealer from Taos

- "'It shouldn't be this hard.' Of course when the relationship is all wrong and you're with the wrong guy this is true, but beware if every time the going gets tough in your relationships, you get going. I've come to realize that walking away may seem hard at the time, but it's always easier to walk than to stick around and work through sensitive, scary issues. Don't be so quick to bail—nobody's going to be perfect, and if the guy is worth fighting for then put in the effort."—Lucy, 38, glass blower, Boulder

### Anything You'd Like to Add?

So there you have five best practices and five worst practices, straight from the dating trenches. You can take the advice or leave it, but it's from battle-tested daters, so think carefully before you dismiss what they have to say.

Now it's your turn. I want you to combine what you picked up from the last two sections, your competitive advice, and the best practices. Right now, right here, I want you to write down five tweaks or changes you could make to your dating approach. This is about reviewing all the best practices you've seen and all the great analysis you've collected to put it all together into a few tweaks you'll make. Again, I'm not suggesting a complete overhaul so that you are not a true version of yourself. Instead, I'm suggesting that small tweaks can add up and go a long way in showing the world the best version of yourself.

Dating Tweak #1 _____

_____

Dating Tweak #2 _____

_____

Dating Tweak #3 _____

_____

Dating Tweak #4 _____

_____

Dating Tweak #5 _____

_____

## Step 5: Implementation

I have good news for you. As a reward for working your way through steps one through four, I'm going to cut you a break for now. This step is all about implementing the great ideas from this chapter. The last thing you want to do is develop all these cool ideas and new thoughts on dating, only to leave them behind as just thoughts and ideas on paper. So just like at work, where you'd jump into implementation, normally that's what I would cover here.

However, there are a few more important additions coming in the next two chapters that will really set you up for success, namely your Spark-It Plan and Recruitment and Affection plan. Both of these chapters will play into your Dating Business Plan, so you get a free pass for now. Think of it as buying four coffees and getting the fifth one free. As your reward for grinding it out in the first four steps, you get to breeze through to the next chapter. Just make sure you've reached your point of arrival before you move on.

## The Bottom Line

You're ready to move on to the next chapter if the following are true:

- You understand the steps a business takes to maneuver through research and development.
- You successfully applied the business concept of research and development to Research and Envelopment.
- You took the time to gather your dating feedback, research the competition, and develop some dating best practices for yourself.

You've reached a milestone at this point and should be proud of yourself. You've made it through Section 1, the Self Assessment. That means you're ready to put what you've learned into action. That's what Section 2, the Action Plan, is all about. You'll learn how to take these great insights about yourself and apply them to a Spark-It Plan, Recruitment and Affection, and Manage-Men.

By the time you finish Section 2, you'll have so many great guys fighting for your affection, you'll wonder why you ever doubted your ability to match your dating success to your business success. So read on! You're about to move many steps closer to landing that great guy you deserve!

section **2**

# The Action Plan

Our transition from Section 1, the Self-Assessment, to Section 2, the Action Plan, is all about the transformation from thinking and planning to taking action and making changes to your dating approach. Here is a crash course on the difference between strategy and action. All you have to do is answer two questions. First, what keeps you up at night? Second, how do you spend your typical day? You will see an example that answers these questions in the form of two pie charts. The first pie chart divvies up the main causes of stress in your life. The second pie chart breaks down how you spend the typical twenty-four hours in your day. You may recall you filled out this same second pie chart about how you spend your typical day in the Opening Remarks section (in a moment, we'll be reviewing that pie chart you completed). As an example, let's take a look at how Beth, a high-performing media executive in New York City, would complete the pie charts. Beth is well regarded by her peers for her creative insights and unflappable determination in front of tough clients. Here are her charts:

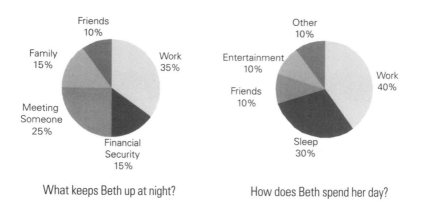

What keeps Beth up at night?

How does Beth spend her day?

"I think work and financial security are related. Five to seven years ago, financial security would have been much higher. However, now that I have enjoyed a few years of moderate success, financially I was able to make a big impact on my long-term plan (owning my own home, retirement fund, etc). However, the downside is that I have a bigger job and more responsibilities, so the pressures at work are a lot more. My pressures with family and friends are primarily around not having enough time with them or making the time I spend with them quality time (especially with my family and aging parents). Since I'm single, my friends play a very important role in my life. I wouldn't be happy and comfortable being single without all my great friends. Of course, I wouldn't mind meeting someone and introducing these great friends to a great guy!"

## What Does It Take to Meet a Great Guy?

So you've seen Beth's pie chart of what keeps her up at night. Right next to it is a second pie chart, this one explaining how she spends her typical day. You can see right away that work and sleep account for 70 percent of Beth's day. The remaining 30 percent is shared among socialization (with friends and family), personal entertainment (reading, watching television), and other (errands, gym, cleaning).

If you know *Dating, Inc.* by now, then you know exactly what I'm going to say here. Where is the time devoted to meeting that great guy? If 15 percent of the anxiety centers upon meeting someone, then why is *zero* percent of the typical time spent trying to meet that person? If your pie chart from the Opening Remarks resembles Beth's, then I'm asking you the same question right now too. This is what Section 2 will cover. We're going to take that super-successful approach you have at work, combine it with all the great self-assessment work you did in Section 1, and turn it into your Dating Action Plan. I know you get excited at work when it's time to execute and get the job done, so keep that same mindset right now as we apply these skills to your dating approach.

## Corporate Memo

TO: All Employees
FROM: Carol Cohen
RE: Your Love Life

Think back to the last time you had a really bad day at the office. You came home, called up your girlfriends and said, "I need a night out with my ladies!" You spend a few hours at the local coffee shop or your favorite restaurant, sipping away while you debrief on the day's events. Your girlfriends listen attentively, commiserating on your work trials and tribulations. You of course feel a lot better, but sooner or later it hits you. What are you going to do about the situation? There's nothing wrong with venting, but you know deep down the whole situation isn't going to go away, no matter how much vodka or coffee you drink. It will only improve when you tackle it, head-on, in your super-savvy business style. Suddenly your confidence kicks in as you realize you can handle it, you will get through it, and you'll be that much stronger for it.

So, think of Part 2, The Action Plan, the same way. As we've mentioned before, there's nothing wrong with commiserating with friends about bad dates. It's only natural to feel better after unloading these negative emotions. But just like at work, if our situation is going to improve, we have to take action. We know how to do it on the job; now we're going to take action and control our dating destinies. So let's get to work!

# chapter **four**

Biz Principle #4:
**Market Plan**

Dating Principle #4:
**Spark-It Plan**

## Agenda

- The role of a company's market plan in attracting great customers
- The role of a Spark-It Plan in attracting great guys
- The four "P's" of a market plan and Spark-It Plan
- Getting ready to get out there

## Work/Life Balance

It's a half hour before your lunch meeting and you're feeling that twinge in your stomach. The morning muffin and coffee have officially worn off. You need a quick bite to make it through the final minutes before your lunch appointment with an important client. Suddenly you remember this new café that just opened across the street from your office. Your mouth waters as you recall seeing their delicious pastries in the window on your way to work today. You decide to take a quick walk over to taste the latest baked delicacies. Thanks to your BlackBerry, you can work while you walk. You won't miss a beat.

Seven minutes later you're parked at a cozy table, BlackBerry in one hand, fresh-baked chocolate-dipped cookie in the other. Your eyes wander from the BlackBerry to the placemat. It's one of those placemats that that doubles as customer entertainment. This one has something for everyone: fun facts, astrology signs, and of course a word jumble. There must have been kids at this table earlier because a small box of crayons sits next to the salt and pepper. You pull out the aqua blue crayon, your favorite color, and take a look at the word jumble:

E K M A   U O Y R   W N O   A T O C I N _____

You sharpen your aqua blue crayon in the cute sharpener on the side of the box and get to work. That familiar Crayola scent starts to bring back great memories of your childhood, when all of a sudden the word jumble quickly catapults you back into your dating mission.

Without giving away your café word jumble, let's just say that this message separates single women who hit their stride in Section 2 of this book from those single women who never get beyond the thoughts, hopes, and desires of Section 1. Knowing you and all that you've accomplished at work, I'll bet you are about to hit your dating stride. Now let's make it happen.

## Every Product or Service Needs a Market

> From: your.boss@work.com
> To: you@work.com
> Subject: Market Plan
> I'm running late agen. we r going 2 need a market plan 4 dis new product.
> Tanks for making it happen.

So why do companies create market plans? In a nutshell, they are created to attract customers and drive sales. Let's say you've manufactured a great new running shoe. You're convinced it's the most stylish and most comfortable running shoe in the marketplace today. You may actually be right, but if you're the only one who knows about it, then why manufacture the running shoe in the first place? This is where the market plan comes in. This is the step where companies figure out how to package up their product or service, price it appropriately, place it in the right stores, and promote it to potential customers.

Let's talk offline for a minute: you see, marketing plans are really all about communication. They are about spreading the gospel of an already great product, or singing the praises of an awesome service. These principles for communication are exactly what we're going to be applying to your dating strategy. Sometimes people hear me talking about marketing products and they immediately say, "Ooh, I hope you're not going to equate single women to products!" Don't worry, I'm not, that would be objectification of women, and my mother raised me better than that. However, there is something to be said for an effective marketing campaign and the messages and ideas it can get across to the right people. By applying these basic marketing strategies to dating, you can learn to enhance and accentuate the best things about the already gorgeous and brilliant you. You can also make sure that these are the first things great guys notice when they are fortunate enough to be in your presence. This will give you the upper hand on the dating scene. When you look your best and feel your best on a date, believe me, you'll rock that date and leave the great guy you're with begging for more. That's what Spark-It Plans do for single women—and it's the same thing a market plan does for companies.

> **JEFF'S DEF•I•NI•TIONS:** According to Wikipedia, a market plan, or marketing plan, is a written document that details the actions necessary to achieve a specified marketing objective(s).

### The Four "P's" of Marketing

Let's break down this whole market plan business into the four key components:

1. **Product:** This is what companies sell to customers. It could be a tangible product, say groceries or a new stereo. Or it could

mean a service, such as a plane ticket to Rome or a health-spa massage.

2. **Place:** This refers to how you get your product into the hands of your customers. It could be an actual store, where customers can shop and see what you have to offer. Or you may be shipping products, meaning customers are buying based on information in a catalog or your Web site.

3. **Price:** This refers to the monetary value placed on the product or service you offer. The goal is to find a price high enough to cover your costs and generate a profit, but low enough to attract sales.

4. **Promotion:** This is how you let potential customers know about the product or service you have to offer. Promotion could include advertising, sales, and discount offers. Anything that spreads the word about your product or service is an example of promotion.

### The Four "P's" of a Widget

For years I've tried to buy a widget. This product has to be the most popular case study in business schools across America. Unfortunately, despite my best efforts, including a full search on eBay, I'm yet to come across even a single widget for sale.

Okay, just kidding, we all know widgets represent a fictional product used to explain a business or economic model. So let's take a quick look at the four "P's" as they relate to widgets to make sure the concept is clear. Then we'll switch over to dating, you'll meet a great guy, and then you, Mr. Right, and the widgets will live happily ever after.

So how might the four "P's" apply to widgets?

1. **Product:** This is an easy one—we're selling widgets. So that's our product. It could be more complicated if we offer a variety of widgets. We might offer different sizes, multiple colors, and so on. But since this is first and foremost a dating and relationship book, let's stick to one product, the basic widget.

2. **Place:** There are multiple ways to get widgets into the hands of our customers. We could cut a deal with local stores to stock widgets on their shelves. We might negotiate a national deal to sell widgets through a retail chain. We also might ship widgets directly to consumers based on orders received from our brochure or Web site.

3. **Price:** Since nobody has ever actually seen a widget, you could argue they're priceless. A real collector's item. But for this book, let's price our widgets at $19.95 or three for $50. That's high enough to cover our costs and make a modest profit, without overpricing our widgets and turning off potential customers.

4. **Promotion:** How might we get customers excited about buying widgets? We could run an advertisement during the hot new prime-time soap of the season. That'll reach 25 million people in one night. It also just might blow our entire annual advertising budget. We could run a cheaper ad in the local newspaper. We'd likely do some market research to find out where our target customers reside. We'd then figure out the best way to spread the word to them about our widgets for sale.

You get the idea. Through product, place, price, and promotion, we've created our product, distributed it, priced it, and notified our potential customers. Those four elements together can take our widgets from the idea phase straight into the hands of our customers. Pretty soon we'll build a widget empire, land on the cover of *Time* magazine, and retire in the Caribbean. As the cool breeze dances across our relaxed bodies, we'll thank the four "P's" for guiding our successful journey straight to Margaritaville.

Snap out of it! You're mind is drifting to piña coladas, Jimmy Buffet songs, and the cool ocean breeze. We've got work to do here, particularly as we now apply the concept of a market plan in business to a Spark-It Plan in dating. You and Mr. Right can jet off to the Caribbean for your honeymoon, after your joint reward and recognition ceremony (a.k.a. wedding).

# From Market to Spark-It

From: your.boss@work.com
To: you@work.com
Subject: Spark-It Plan
I'm running late agen. we r going 2 need a spark-it plan 4 u to find dat grate guy.
Tanks for making it happen

If the thought of marketing yourself to land great guys scared you before this chapter began, hopefully our widget example helped put it in perspective. Whether or not you've held an actual job in marketing, you've already been exposed to the four "P's" of marketing for years as a customer. So I know that as a super-smart, go-getter single woman, you've got a good grasp of the concept even as a target customer. Now let's pretend your boss changed the e-mail ever so slightly and now wants you to create a Spark-It Plan to land that great guy. Keep that same business mindset, and we'll be through this and on to dating victory in no time.

**JEFF'S DEF•I•NI•TIONS:** According to *Dating, Inc.*, a Spark-It Plan is a written document that details the actions necessary for a woman to achieve a specified dating objective(s).

## Corporate Memo

TO: All Employees
FROM: Carol Cohen
RE: Your Love Life

Notice Jeff left pricing out of the equation above. There's one great reason for this omission. When you combine pricing with dating, people think you're talking about prostitution. We would never want to leave you thinking anything like that! You'll find out later in this chapter that the business concept of pricing in marketing when applied to dating will be discussed as the "price" you'll pay for not changing your dating approach. It's a small stretch, but work with us on this one since we know you'll appreciate the overall lessons.

## Your Personal Brand

Okay, thinking about branding yourself might feel a bit strange, unless you're Madonna, but in reality, you do this each and every day when you determine what you need to do to put your best foot forward. You especially do this in business. When you have an important meeting or presentation, I'll bet you spend days preparing your talking points and picking just the right outfit. The same care of preparation and enthusiasm can absolutely translate into dating.

So going forward in this chapter, instead of using the term "product," we're going to say "personal brand." This will be our understanding together that we're talking about tips and tools to put forth the best possible version of yourself on the singles scene.

### Diversity Will Overcome Adversity

When you think about your personal brand and using it to meet that great guy, remember this advice from Alex, a money manager in Tokyo, Japan. He's recently engaged and offers the importance of diversity as it relates to dating:

"Investing in many relationships (friends, family, etc.) can strengthen your romantic relationships. Diversification keeps you from requiring one person to meet all of your needs. In a business setting, diversification allows a business to endure downturns in particular markets and to benefit from a variety of opportunities. You can do the same in your dating approach."

Hey, if you remember nothing else from this quote, remember the word "diversification." That one word can keep your stock portfolio balanced, and it can do the same for your portfolio of men to date.

### So What Is My Personal Brand?

Here's where your hard work in the previous chapters will come in handy. You didn't think I'd make you do all that hard work for nothing, did you? In a moment, we'll circle back to roll together all of the work you did on dating goals, milestones, and personality strengths and opportunities. But first, let's have a little fun together. Here's a brief five-question quiz that can help you define your personal brand. Simply circle the answer that best describes you:

Question #1:
**When I'm at a party, you're most likely to find me:**
   a.  Sitting in the corner sipping on a mixed drink or glass of juice.
   b.  Hanging out primarily with the friend who came to the party with me.
   c.  Mingling with the crowd, talking to various people.
   d.  I'm the life of the party, everyone will know my name by night's end.

Question #2:
**When it comes to fashion, you'll most likely find me dressed in:**
   a.  The latest fashion trends from top-notch designers.
   b.  Sharp-looking clothes, but not necessarily this season's latest designs.
   c.  The clothes do not make the woman, it shouldn't matter what I wear.
   d.  Jeans and a sweatshirt—comfort before fashion!

Question #3:
**When stress enters a relationship, my most likely reaction is:**
   a.  You've got to face stress head-on and deal with it right away.
   b.  I'm hoping my boyfriend can lead the charge in dealing with it.
   c.  I'm such a calm type, stress rarely gets to me.
   d.  If I ignore it long enough, maybe it will go away.

Question #4
**When it comes to Valentine's Day in a relationship, here's my ideal way to celebrate with my man:**

 a.  Valentine's Day is overrated, it should be treated like any other day.
 b.  A card and some chocolate would be nice, but nothing special required.
 c.  Let's go for the romantic night—candlelight dinner, flowers, an intimate evening together, and some fun between the sheets.
 d.  Valentine's Day is the single most important day of the year for any relationship. I really want my man to pull out all the stops and truly make me feel special.

Question #5:
**How would you describe your communication style in relationships:**

 a.  I'm the quiet type, communication isn't really my thing.
 b.  I'll tackle a tough dating subject if I have to, but coasting is my preferred relationship style.
 c.  Communication is a real strength for me, everyone I've ever dated and all my friends always say I really know how to communicate with people.
 d.  I've got a bit of a "fire-in-the-belly" and that can make it tough to communicate with me because I've been known to get worked up over small things.

### Tell Me More, What's My Score?

Have no fear, I'm not going to ask you to add together your "A" responses, subtract the "D" responses, and divide by the sum total of "B" and "C" answers. The reasons I asked these five questions is because there is no right answer to a personal brand. We're all unique, and there's something special about each of us on the dating scene. Something that makes you worthy of a great guy. But that something is different for everyone. If you're the quiet one at parties who likes to wear jeans, coast through relationships, and rarely gets stressed, you will offer a completely different personal brand from the fire-in-the-belly "fashionista" who likes all the stops pulled out for Valentine's Day. Neither approach is right; they're just different. So look back at your five answers, think about them together, and get a sense of the person it describes. This is the first step to understanding your personal brand.

---

### Corporate Memo

TO: All Employees
FROM: Carol Cohen
RE: Your Love Life

---

Personal brands are so important at work. Think about those successful women in business whom you really respect, particularly the ones in the high-powered positions. How would you describe their personal brand? I'll bet you see traits like confidence, leadership abilities, strategic thinking, and an ability to execute. This personal brand did not happen overnight—it was a conscious decision by these women to portray this kind of demeanor in the office. There's no reason single women can't apply the same principle to dating. Think about a single friend you really admire (or someone in a successful relationship). How do they carry themselves around men? What aspects of their personality could you add to round out your dating skills?

---

### Time to Check Your Homework

I would never suggest a quiz on its own is enough to build your personal brand. The bulk of it should come from the great work you did in past chapters. Do you remember that Dating Business Plan you've been building? Now's the time to look at it again because it holds the keys to your personal brand. I want you to specifically look at these elements:

- Dating Souls and Objectives
- Dating strengths and weaknesses as identified by you, your friends/family, ex-partners, and your target guy
- Dating tweaks

This great work you put in earlier, plus your responses to the quiz, is where your personal brand lies. This is the secret to the kind of person you are and could be when it comes to dating and relationships. So how do you put it all together? It comes down to answering three important questions (don't worry about answering them just yet, but get ready because that time will come in a few more paragraphs):

**Question #1:** Which dating strengths do I want to further highlight and display on the dating scene?

**Question #2:** Which dating areas do I want to improve to increase my success on the dating scene?

**Question #3:** How can I turn my "dating tweaks" into my strengths on the dating scene?

Put the answers to these three questions together and you have the strengths to show, the opportunities to improve, and the behaviors to modify. Together, this forms the basis of your personal brand, or how you want to be perceived on the dating scene.

### *Commit to Your Personal Brand*

You've taken the quiz, reviewed your hard work from earlier chapters, and answered the three questions. Now it's time to actually put it all together and describe the person you plan to be on the dating scene. Again, this is not personality overhaul time. Notice we're only talking about letting your strengths shine through and improving or modifying some of your dating turnoffs. This is not about becoming someone you're not. Remember, a great guy is going to love the real you. But while your search is on, you can certainly work toward showing the best possible version of yourself.

Let's talk offline for a minute: I know it probably scares you a bit to think about making some of these dating tweaks. We all get scared when we face obstacles. Still, that doesn't have to stop you in your tracks. It's like my father-in-law Victor always says, "When you see an obstacle in your path, you don't let it stop you, you use it as a stepping stone." I've used that advice at work, in relationships, and whenever a tough challenge is staring me in the face. It's empowering, don't you think? At the very least, I dropped in a quote from my father-in-law and that's got to put me in good graces the next time I see him.

So put it all together right here, right now, and describe the person you'll be on the dating scene. But before you do, how about one sample to bring the idea of a personal brand to life. Meet Veronica. She's a thirty-six-year-old event planner from New Hampshire. Coming off a tough breakup after three years with the guy she thought she'd marry, Veronica is ready to make some changes and get it right. Here's how she describes her personal brand:

"Being a giver and showing trust are two of my greatest qualities, but sometimes I go too far. My failed relationship with Stephen is a case in point. He ended up cheating on me while my trusting nature continuously gave him the benefit of the doubt. I'm going to hold my own better in relationships. I like my clothes and hair but my best friend Becky always tells me I'd look cuter with a shorter style. I'm going to give that a try and see what happens . . . "

Veronica had a lot more to say on her personal brand. I wanted to show you one personality tweak and one appearance tweak she plans to make. That's what we're talking about here. Little changes that can add up to a big difference.

Now it's your turn. Put pen (or pencil) to paper and tell me exactly the person you'll be going forward on the dating scene with your Personal Brand:

_____

_____

_____

_____

Don't think of your personal brand as a static definition. Whatever you've just written should be a changing, fluid description. Brands in business rarely stay exactly the same forever. They adapt based on market conditions and customer feedback. Remember the product launch debacle that was New Coke? And the brilliant brand revamp of Coca-Cola Classic? Your personal brand is a great starting point, but you definitely want to revisit it from time to time and make tweaks as necessary. Remember, I'm not asking you to be a different person every night. Instead, check in with yourself every once in awhile, get back to what you really want in a guy and whether you're properly communicating that goal. Ask yourself and maybe even a few of those people you trust what's working and what's not. Ask yourself if the personal brand you are portraying is the best possible version of yourself and is effectively communicating how wonderful you are for all the world to see.

## The Price You'll Pay

The second "P" in the marketing mix is price. Earlier in this chapter we talked about thinking of price as the "price you'll pay" if you don't make any changes to your dating approach. So that's a question you need to ask yourself. Over the years you've had a dating approach. If you choose to make no changes after reading this book, then you'll continue to rely on that same dating approach. To me, that means that the price you'll pay is continuing to get the same results you've been getting. If that's not a fate you want, then now is the time to say enough is enough. I'm going to become the person I've been building in *Dating, Inc.* That's the proactive person I was born to be and it's the dater I'm going to become. I deserve it, and so does the great guy I'm going to meet.

### · · · state of the business #4 · · · · · · · · · · · · · ·

Women in the U.S. workforce earn 79.5 percent as much as men. So there's still a wage gap, but their earnings are up from 62.5 percent of men's in 1979. Women have made such great strides in the workforce, now let's get the same positive results in dating and relationships!

## Location, Location, Location

The third "P" is all about the place, or location. In business, your offerings need to be on the right shelves or known by the right people to reach your target customer. That's how you cast a wide net in the marketplace. In dating, "place" means where you need to be to land the great guys. Another great business analogy that plays into place is the concept of "Employer of Choice." According to the Society of Human Resources Management, a company becomes an Employer of Choice when "overall work conditions have enabled a company to successfully attract and retain talent because employees choose to work there."

Translate this to the dating world, and the question becomes this: How can you become a Dater of Choice for single guys? You've got it all. You're smart, successful, and fabulous, what a catch! So, what's the best way to get the word out to great guys that you're a *Dater of Choice*? We turned to our SuperStar Network of single men and women and those in relationships to answer this question. Here are their top three thoughts and views on becoming a Dater of Choice for single guys:

1. "Be yourself . . . with a twist! Never be something that you're not, but there's nothing wrong with adding a hint of mystery

or excitement to your everyday persona."—Wanda, 33, tech consultant from Denver, Colorado.

2. "Let the guy take the lead at times for tradition. I'm a feminist, don't get me wrong! But sometimes it's fun to let him hold the door for me, or help me out of the car. But don't be afraid to step up and take control at times too!"—Mandy, 42, receptionist from Greensboro, North Carolina.

3. "Stay away from games and sex on first dates. Games get old fast and quick sex ends relationships fast."—Patricia, 26, dental technician from Bozeman, Montana.

### Reinforce to Stay the Course

Beyond the three tips, Noel, a twenty-four-year-old marketing assistant working in southern France, brought up the idea of positive reinforcement to draw in great partners:

*"Positive reinforcement is always a good motivator. I believe that most people inherently like making others happy if they can. This is particularly true if a man is interested in a woman. So being appreciative and complimentary when men do great things is bound to lead to great results. Some people think that being coy and 'hard to get' increases their attractiveness—and some people like the 'chase.' However, my thought is that fascination with the unattainable tends to be a short-term proposition. It's only intriguing for so long, and then the guy gets bored with the challenge."*

### From Devotion to Promotion

I've got great news for you! To reward you for mastering three of the four "P's," I'm going to cut you a break on the fourth "P," promotion. It's not just because I'm a nice guy, although I'd like to believe that has something to do with it. Rather, I don't want to step on the toes of the juicy material about to come your way in the Recruitment and Affection chapter. That's where we really get into the nuts and bolts of attracting a great guy. As you can imagine, that's pretty close to the concept of promotion. So instead of giving an overview of how to promote yourself to land great guys, I'm going to tell you that if you wanted that information, it's right around the corner in the next chapter. You're about to learn exactly how a recruitment strategy at work can be applied to land a great guy on the singles scene. So get ready to take those first steps toward total dating satisfaction.

## The Bottom Line

You're ready to move on to the next chapter if the following is true:

- You understand the four "P's" of marketing.
- You created your personal brand and feel comfortable with that person.
- You are truly ready to take those first big steps toward meeting a great guy.

# chapter
# five

Biz Principle #5:
**Recruitment and Selection**

Dating Principle #5:
**Recruitment and Affection**

## Agenda

- The definition of recruitment and selection
- How companies approach finding the right person for each job
- How recruitment and selection in the business world translates into Recruitment and Affection in the dating world
- How to find your ideal type for first and second dates using a Recruitment and Affection plan
- How to make the decision after first dates whether to grant second dates and beyond

## Work/Life Balance

You've got a big lunch today. One of your top clients is visiting from out of town and it's your job to schmooze him over a delicious meal at the local steak house. There's a lot riding on this lunch, and your boss knows you're the one to trust. You fire off a few last e-mails before logging off and heading out to meet your client. Stepping into the elevator, your mind is swirling with facts and figures to share at lunch. You've prepared for two weeks for this moment and you just know you're going to nail it.

You barely notice the elderly gentlemen sharing the elevator with you. He gives you a quick nod and then turns back to the newspaper spread open before him. Your focus remains on the big lunch meeting, but out of the corner of your eye you notice the back page of the newspaper. In the top right corner is a word jumble and you just can't help but solve it:

O G  D F N I  O R U Y  N M A _____

I'm hoping this word jumble can become your mantra for this chapter. This is officially the point in *Dating, Inc.* where the search begins for your terrific man. We've laid out practical, applicable theory and we've talked about becoming the best version of yourself. Now is the time to put it all together, get out there, and take some action. I know you can execute on the job—you wouldn't be a SuperStar at work without that skill. Now go out there and do the same for your dating life. That great guy is just waiting to be met. He's all yours. So go out and find him.

## Recruitment and Selection at Work

From: your.boss@work.com
To: you@work.com
Subject: New Marketing Analyst
I got 30 secs b4 a meeting. i want u to find a new marketing analyst. can u put tgthr some ideas by 5 o'clok and leeve em on my desk.
Tanks for making it happen.

Do you remember this e-mail from the intro chapter? This was your boss's way of telling you to go out and find a great marketing analyst. Despite the cryptic abbreviations, we talked about how you could execute on this plan. Now that we're officially in the recruitment and selection chapter, let's break it down even further.

**JEFF'S DEF•I•NI•TIONS:** According to the Society for Human
Resource Management, recruitment refers to "the practice of soliciting
and actively seeking applicants to fill recently vacated or newly created
positions using a variety of methods."

A typical corporate recruitment and selection plan has five steps:

1. Job description: How would a company describe the position
   they're filling?
2. Key qualifications: What qualities should a candidate possess?
3. Recruitment strategy: Where can the best candidates be found?
4. Interviews: How do the candidates come across in person?
5. Offer: Who is the best choice for the job?

### Our Cupid Speaks

If you read the acknowledgments section of this book, you learned
that Carol and I were introduced by the head of recruitment and selection at American Express. Her name is Marietta Cozzi, and she truly
is our Cupid. Her matchmaking skills, along with those of Deb Foley
(who secured a second date for us by exchanging our phone numbers),
changed our lives forever. We also like to point out that Marietta specifically "recruited and selected" us for each other. She then taught me
the business skill to put together a retention plan to keep Carol interested during our courtship (but that's a story for another day)!

How could we possibly get through the recruitment and selection
chapter without calling on our Cupid, Marietta, to share her expertise as
a vice president of recruitment and selection? Here's Marietta's take on
what makes for a great recruitment and selection plan at a company:

"The keys to the most successful recruitment and selection strategy
are an employment branding campaign, easy-to-understand position
descriptions, using technology to enable the process, and remembering
that relationships are still the most important ingredient for recruitment. Each of these, especially the personal branding and relationship
aspects, are very important. In the world of recruitment (regardless of
the size of the company), relationship building is still the most critical

portion of finding and securing the hire. Even with technology, personal networking is still very important. If you take all these strategies and switch recruitment and selection in business with Recruitment and Affection in *Dating, Inc.*, you can apply all the same techniques to be successful in your search for a new partner."

You've got to love Marietta. She knows her matchmaking and her business. It's no wonder she's such a dynamo when it comes to attracting and hiring the best possible person for the job! While we had her attention, we figured we would get you a free tip on the business side of recruitment and selection. Hey, we know this is a dating book, but high-performing, successful businesswomen can always add a business tip or two. So if you're reading this book to land a great guy, but just happen to be in the market for a great new job, here's Marietta's take on what you can do to master the job search and land the right job:

"The first piece of advice is to do your research about the industry, company, department and position you are interested in. The next piece of advice is about networking and how far you can extend your network . . . neighbors, relatives, former college friends, church, other organizational connections, commuting buddies, etc. Get the word out and let people know that you are looking. I would, again, suggest similar advice to someone about to look for a new guy to date. Potential connections exist with nearly every interaction you have."

Do you see that? Even in giving job search advice, Marietta knows exactly how to cross over and explain the correlation to dating. She really is a matchmaker. By the way, if you're looking for love and a new job, we can give you her phone number. You're okay with that, right Marietta?

## What Is a Recruitment and Affection Plan?

From: your.boss@work.com
To: you@work.com
Subject: Getting Married
I got 30 secs b4 a meeting. i want u to find a spouse.
can u put tgthr some ideas by 5 o'clok and leeve em
on my desk.
Tanks for making it happen.

While recruitment and selection is all about finding the best person for the job, Recruitment and Affection is about finding the right man for your relationship.

**JEFF'S DEF•I•NI•TIONS:** According to *Dating, Inc.*, Recruitment and Affection refers to the practice of actively seeking men to fill recently vacated or newly created relationship openings using a variety of methods.

I know we're switching over from "biz-speak" to "love-speak" now and it's okay if that overwhelms you or even scares you a bit. Remember, though, that you're a smart, capable all-star at work and if you had to, you would know exactly how to recruit and select a great candidate for a job. That means you already have the skill set to find a great guy too. All I'm going to do now is help you translate a skill you've already learned into the romance arena. We're going to take skills you already know logically and apply them to a matter of the heart.

## Corporate Memo

TO: All Employees
FROM: Carol Cohen
RE: Your Love Life

Emotion versus logic is so powerful in decision-making. Whenever I'm filling an open position at work, I'm able to approach it logically. I ask questions like "What are the ideal skills for this job?" and "Where can I find the most qualified candidates?" I would never get caught up in emotional questions like "I wonder whether or not the candidates will like me?"

That's what this chapter is all about. You take those logical thoughts that guide you to good decisions in hiring employees and simply apply them to a new arena—finding your fabulous soul mate. Knowing that you already have the skills will hopefully help turn any fear or apprehension you may be feeling into excitement for what is ahead!

# Emotion Versus Logic

Carol raises a great point in her column. Emotion and logic are so tricky. Work is so much easier to approach logically. Then you turn to dating and relationships, and all these "feelings" creep in. Now as we've discussed, I'm not advocating getting rid of emotion entirely. I hope that when you logically find this great guy, you'll let all those gushy-gooey feelings flood back in to your brain, to help your heart decide whether he's right for you. But if you're currently letting emotion completely rule your approach to dating, I'm hoping you won't spend another precious minute allowing your smart, savvy mind to go there. Trying to make your dating decisions strictly based on emotion can paralyze you and turn you into an ice-cream-scooping, *Sex-and-the-City*-watching bachelorette-for-life.

I'm here to tell you it doesn't have to be that way. *Don't* completely drop emotion from the equation. *Do* let logic and those sound business skills you possess take the lead. Believe me, once we have your plan in place, you'll have so many guys flocking to you, you'll need some emotions just to weed out the bad, or even just okay, seeds.

Look, I know there will be nights where you just want to grab a drink or coffee with your girlfriends and vent about a bad date or guy who's just not right for you. Believe me, there's nothing wrong with that, and guys do it all the time too! But in this chapter we're going to talk implementation, execution, and getting the job done. That's what will get you out there, meeting lots of prospects, and what will ultimately find the perfect guy for you.

## The Five Steps Applied to Recruitment and Affection

Just as a recruitment and selection plan has five key steps, so does the Recruitment and Affection plan:

1. **Description of the guy:** How would you describe the ideal man you're looking for? Are you looking for a one-night-stand bedmate or a lifetime-of-love soul mate?

2. **Key characteristics:** What qualities or traits should he have to be considered for a date? Is it more important that he looks like Tom Cruise or makes you laugh like Jerry Seinfeld?

3. **Recruitment and Affection strategy:** Where is the best place to find the right guys? Should you be looking in the wine bar around the corner, or the corner market?

4. **First dates:** How can you put yourself in a position to land dates with these guys? Are you willing to go on enough bad first dates for the shot at great second dates?

5. **Second dates and beyond:** When one great guy emerges from the pack, how are you going to secure a second date, and maybe more?

---

## Corporate Memo

TO: All Employees
FROM: Carol Cohen
RE: Your Love Life

---

I know I've said this before, but it's really worth repeating to drive home the point. We are smart, strong, successful women, and commiserating about bad dates and relationships is an important part of feeling supported. However, a great idea isn't worth nearly as much if it isn't implemented! By thinking logically first, and focusing on implementation, we can take control of our dating destinies.

Think about it. If your boss at work asked you to roll out a new product, implementation would be critical. Of course, a few nights commiserating with your colleagues about product obstacles and challenges are natural, but it won't get the job done. Ultimately, we get good results at work based on how well and efficiently we implement our great ideas. Why can't we have the same approach in dating?

---

### Women's Intuition

Women have come a long way in the workplace. They've landed top jobs and made great strides in closing the gender salary gap. But according to Marisa, a physical therapist in Wisconsin, there's work to be done in dating and relationships, too:

"I give my all at work. I feel so empowered. When something needs to get done, I just roll up my sleeves and make it happen. But in relationships we've been conditioned by society to not feel empowered, to just wait for our Prince Charming. Then, when we do supposedly get swept off our feet by our prince, we're expected to be so perfect and pretty. When you think about it, as women we've worked so hard to be empowered in the workforce. Now's the time to do the same in relationships!

## Break It Down for Me

Let's look in greater detail at the five steps that make up a Recruitment and Affection plan.

### Step 1—Description of Your Guy

Let's start with a general write-up about your desired guy. It would be helpful to refer back to your Wishin' Statement from Chapter 1. This is where you first described your dream guy.

Just as a refresher, you're an ambitious woman who deserves the best, and I know that because of this, you might be tempted to say "tall, dark, and handsome, with a Harvard M.B.A., independently wealthy, funnier than Seinfeld, and without a flaw." Remember, though, we're not talking about perfection here—no man is 100 percent perfect, and if you set out to find someone who fits that bill, you'll be setting yourself up for failure. Instead, we're talking about the "need-to-have" versus "nice-to-have" qualities that you desire. In life, as in business, it's important to set reasonable, attainable goals to achieve success.

And please remember, "set reasonable goals" does not mean "settling for just anyone." I'm just asking you to be honest and realize there are no perfect men out there. What I am saying is that you want to be clear on the qualities that really matter to you in a relationship. This is also a great opportunity to reread that Wishin' Statement and see if it still describes the person you're looking for. Your thoughts may have shifted as you've delved deeper into the *Dating, Inc.* plan. So take a moment, reread that Wishin' Statement, and make sure this really is the ideal guy you're going after.

### Step 2—Key Characteristics

Now that you have a description of him, it's time to get more specific. In Chapter 2, Souls and Objectives, you provided detail on the kind of man you are looking for. Now is the time to refer back to that description and refresh your memory of your dream guy. As you can see, your Recruitment and Affection plan starts easy. You get to use some of your hard work from the previous chapters.

Just remember what we said in the Souls and Objectives chapter about too many qualities under your must-have, nice-to-have, or who-cares chart. If your chart has too many must-haves, are you being realistic? On the flip side, if your chart is full of who-cares responses, you run the risk of dating down. The key is that you combine your Wishin' Statement with your must-have, nice-to-have, and who-cares chart to formulate a truly clear picture of the guy you're going after and the traits he possesses.

### Step 3—Recruitment and Affection Strategy

At this point you have a description of the guy and the more in-depth details that would make him your ideal mate. Now it's time to take some action. But before we jump into step three, I want you to congratulate yourself again. You're cruising now, really showing a desire to improve your approach. Believe me, this new way of thinking is going to pay off in finding a guy who deserves to be with you.

This is the kind of thinking that leads to recruiting top-quality candidates for an organization and top-notch contenders for a relationship. If we were talking about an open job, at this point you would have the description of the position and in-depth details of the skills and qualifications. Thanks to your new business approach to dating, you're at the same point in your new way of thinking about relationships.

Now, let's turn our attention to step three. I really want you to focus on the word "action" because it's the key at this point. I can't tell you how many single women cruise through steps one and two, only to grind to a halt on step three. It's probably because steps one and two only require writing, whereas step three requires action.

---

## Corporate Memo

TO: All Employees
FROM: Carol Cohen
RE: Your Love Life

---

At this point, it's important to think about the role confidence plays in getting what you want, both in business and in dating. At work, we've all seen how clients flock to the sales person who appears confident. There's something about that successful demeanor that makes clients want to do business with you.

The same holds true in dating. You have that description of your ideal husband; now it's time to show the confidence it takes to go out there and find him. If we can do it at the office, there's no reason we can't duplicate that confident appearance on the singles scene. By now, I hope you've come to realize that when smart women like you, all across the globe, can succeed at work, then you can absolutely succeed in dating!

---

### I'm Ready to Take Some Action, Now Where Do I Find My Top-Notch Guy?

Where do you actually find a great guy who meets all the important criteria? It may seem like a huge enigma to find one great guy among the sea of average guys, but why not think strategically about it? In business, it's important to stay on top of what your professional peers are doing, and in many cases, model their best practices, so as to achieve similar results. Here's how you can do that in love.

I want you to think about your five closest girlfriends who are in relationships. Write down their names and exactly how they met their boyfriend, partner, or husband.

Friend #1 is _____ and here's how she met her guy:

_____

Friend #2 is _____ and here's how she met her guy:

_____

Friend #3 is _____ and here's how she met her guy:

_____

Friend #4 is _____ and here's how she met her guy:

_____

Friend #5 is _____ and here's how she met her guy:

_____

Right away you've got five great strategies to meet someone new! Plus, you know these strategies have worked for your friends.

### Women's Intuition

We asked a happily married member of our SuperStar Network to answer just this question about how her five closest friends met. Her name is Judy. She's been married four years and works as a personal trainer in Manchester, England:

*"Five of my friends and family members met in the following ways:*

1. *Introduced by me at work (they're married)*
2. *Met at a wedding (they're married)*
3. *Met in a class at their university (they're engaged)*
4. *Met in a pub (they're married)*
5. *Met through online dating (they're engaged)*

*Some of the other places I think people could meet are at a gym, although if things don't work out (no pun intended) you will probably continue to see this person, on a holiday vacation, at a restaurant, coffeehouse, on a blind date, singles events, or a co-ed sports team—the options really are endless. Believe it or not, I met my last boyfriend (before my husband) on an airplane. I guess love was in the air!"*

**action item** ✓

{ If you were thinking about filling an open position, you would now think about the best places to find quality candidates. Take that same drive for results and enthusiasm to get the job done at work and do the same right now for your love life. Where do you find that special someone you described? Let me help you out a bit. Here's a list of the twenty-two most common ways that people have told me they met someone special:

- Online dating
- Matchmaking services
- Charitable organizations
- Places of worship
- Singles vacations
- School
- Parties
- Seminar or class
- Dinner gatherings
- Laundromat
- Music concert

- Speed dating
- Blind dates and setups
- Volunteer work
- Summer cottage/ski houses
- Workplace
- Coffee shop
- Bars, pubs, and clubs
- Gym
- Local bookstore
- Zoo
- Museum }

## You Know You Better Than I Know You

You know better than I do the kind of man you're looking for. Do any of the items on the list jump out to you as great places to find your guy? If some of these ideas scare you a bit, then choose the least intimidating options. By starting easy, you'll build some positive momentum, and then you can move on to the more challenging ideas.

Don't be afraid to expand this list. It's just a starting point (and in a moment I'll be asking you to commit to at least five new recruitment ideas). Feel free to use some of my ideas, but add the ones that match best with your personality, and even include some ideas from friends and family. The goal here is to put yourself in the places and situations most likely to be frequented by the guy you're trying to meet. The more often you get out there and put yourself in those situations and places, the higher your chances of coming across your dream guy. In this step, all we're trying to do is increase your odds that we can get you in the same room with him. In the next step, we'll figure out what to do when you find him.

If you're struggling to figure out how to best use these dating meeting places to your advantage, here are three examples of strategies based on the list above:

1. **Online dating**—You may be thinking of joining a top online dating site like Yahoo!Personals, which is fantastic given their high success rates. You could also pick a second specialized site based on your individual dating needs (i.e., something that meets one of your "must haves" from the key characteristics chart). For example, if you are Christian and really want to find someone with similar religious beliefs, you could join e-ChristianDating.com to improve your odds of dating another Christian person.

2. **Seminar or class**—You may have always wanted to take a particular painting class or writing course. Before you sign up, ask yourself whether your ideal guy would likely be taking this class too. If yes, go ahead and sign up. If not, think about a secondary class you're interested in that gives you better odds of finding your ideal guy.

3. **Charitable organization**—Perhaps you love reading to disadvantaged children or calling out bingo numbers at the retirement community. These are certainly noble causes, but you could also pick a more social organization, one that would have multiple volunteers on assignment, such as constructing homes for the needy. You'll be giving back to the community while improving your chances of meeting another giving person.

### It's Your Turn to Let the Ideas Churn

Right here, right now, commit to five new steps you'll take to meet a great guy. As I said before, feel free to borrow from the examples shared in this chapter. Or come up with your own. The important thing is that you commit to making it happen:

1. New Dating Recruitment Step #1 is _____

   _____

2. New Dating Recruitment Step #2 is _____

   _____

3. New Dating Recruitment Step #3 is _____

   _____

4. New Dating Recruitment Step #4 is _____

   _____

5. New Dating Recruitment Step #5 is _____

   _____

## Step 4—It's Your First Date, Don't Be Late

When you interview candidates for a job, you rarely just give an offer to the first candidate who walks through your door, no matter how perfect and poised they may seem. You need to meet a few prospects before you settle on the best choice.

After all, you are worth it, and you deserve the best choice. Never forget that point. Just because you haven't met your ideal mate yet doesn't mean that I want you to settle for the first guy that comes along. Once you master the strategies in this book, you'll have so many great guys knocking down your door, you won't be able to handle the influx of potential partners.

Sizing up prospects for a job works the same in dating. This is where you decide who the best match is for a second date. It's similar to work, where you would screen a dozen candidates for a job and then invite back only a handful for a second round interview.

I know that you're confident and secure at the office; now, I want you to feel confident during this dating process too. That's why I've put together a list of the top ten mistakes single women make during the early dating phase to help you along this journey. Remember, any one of these mistakes has the potential to land you in a relationship with the wrong guy.

## The Top Ten Mistakes to Avoid in the Early Stages of Dating

**1.** Settling for the first guy that comes along just to be in a relationship.

**2.** Pretending there's chemistry and overlooking a deal breaker.

**3.** Playing games with a great guy just to keep the upper hand.

**4.** Letting close friends and family decide your fate with a man.

**5.** Missing the signs that He's Just Not That Into You.

**6.** Getting drunk on a first date and making a fool of yourself.

**7.** Sleeping with a guy on the first date.

**8.** Going on serial first dates without looking for Mr. Right.

**9.** Turning down a date instead of taking a chance.

**10.** Sitting in your apartment and avoiding dating entirely.

Think about how this top-ten list would translate into an interview situation. Imagine if you settled for the first candidate you interviewed, pretended a bad candidate was a good candidate, or played games with a great candidate, just for kicks. None of that would fly in the business world, and it shouldn't be your approach in dating. We'll get into this concept in greater detail in the Manage-Men chapter, coming up.

---

### Corporate Memo

TO: All Employees
FROM: Carol Cohen
RE: Your Love Life

---

We've all dated the wrong guy. The one who treats women terribly, cancels on dates, or even has some other woman that he's stringing along on the side. But would any of us tolerate such inappropriate behavior from an employee? Remember, the goal in dating, as in business, is to surround yourself with the right people who will enhance your life. Every day you spend with the wrong guy is another day you're missing out in your search for the right guy.

Pay attention to those signs if you're getting a bad vibe about a guy. Have you ever felt a strange vibe at the office and used good gut instincts or intuition to end a working relationship or uncover wrongdoings and fire an employee? Women in business rely on gut instinct all the time. So why ignore it when it comes to dating? Use that same intuition that guides you at work to make decisions about whether you're dating the right guy.

I know it's tough to end a relationship or admit it's not working out. But if an employee wasn't working out at your company—not performing or behaving inappropriately, or generally not contributing to the overall vision and values of the business—you wouldn't hesitate to fire him or her, right? Finding the courage to do the same in your personal life is key to keeping your forward momentum. So look yourself in the mirror and find that honest place that tells you when it's time to move on.

Let me say this again: I know it's not easy to admit you're with the wrong guy. I've defended horrible guys to my best friends, my sister, even my parents. Starting over just seemed so difficult. I kept thinking, "Things will get better if I just stick it out." But they never get better with the wrong person. It took me a long time to realize this fact, but it is so powerful to finally realize that trying to make the wrong relationship work is in fact worse than being alone and searching for a better guy.

---

## Step 5—Second Dates and Beyond

Think of this step as giving an offer to the best candidate in an interview. We're not talking about engagement and marriage. All we're talking about here is plucking out the best guy from all the first dates and agreeing to more dates. This might mean:

- Agreeing to second, third, and fourth dates
- Deciding if you want to take yourself off the market and give it a go
- Making your feelings known to the other person and seeing if they're reciprocated

Let me give you some insight here into what a man is looking for at this stage. Contrary to what others might say, there's nothing wrong with making your feelings known to a guy and admitting that you're having a great time so far. Sure, players will see this as an unwanted commitment coming their way, but who wants to date a guy like that anyway? The right men will actually be flattered by your honesty, especially if they reciprocate those feelings! More on this to come in the Manage-Men chapter too (you don't want me to give you all my best tips too soon, do you)?

---

## Corporate Memo

TO: All Employees
FROM: Carol Cohen
RE: Your Love Life

---

Do you remember earlier in the chapter when we talked about compromises in negotiations? Well, another important strategy in any good negotiation is to never fully reveal all your cards too early in the discussion. You have to leave a little something in your pocket or there's no wiggle room when negotiations get tight. As Denise, one of our SuperStar Network businesswomen points out, "The key to a successful negotiation is understanding where the other person is coming from and letting them talk about what's important to them so you can find some middle ground."

So you need to leave a little on the table in dating. Expressing a few sentiments early on is definitely okay. That's what helps a relationship progress from those early dates into something more serious. However, there's no reason to lay it all on the table this early and tell the guy everything you're thinking and feeling. It could turn off a negotiator in the early stages of the deal and just might do the same to a great guy.

If you've played your cards right, you'll have tons of magnificent, top-of-the-class men to consider for second dates.

---

### *Rolling Right Along*

That leads us right into the next chapter, Management—or, for the purposes of *Dating, Inc.*, Manage-Men. Here you'll learn how to make a great impression on first dates and make terrific guys beg for a second date and beyond. In other words, we'll be going into greater detail on steps four and five in the Recruitment and Affection plan.

# The Bottom Line

You're ready to move on to the next chapter if the following are true:

- You understand the meaning of recruitment and selection.
- You know how to apply recruitment and selection in the business world to Recruitment and Affection in personal relationships.
- You mapped out the characteristics that are important to you in finding a man versus those you can live without.
- You have developed your own Recruitment and Affection plan to strategically use with the men you want to meet.
- You learned winning strategies and planned great places to meet new people.

# chapter
# six

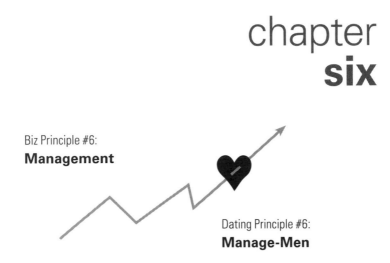

Biz Principle #6:
**Management**

Dating Principle #6:
**Manage-Men**

## Agenda

- The importance of people management in leading employees
- How managing people in organizations translates into managing men in relationships
- What it takes to consistently have an influx of great guys coming into your life
- How to conduct early assessments of guys you're meeting to decide whether or not to continue investing time in them
- The best ways to reward great dating behaviors from guys to keep those great behaviors coming

## Work/Life Balance

Now that was a great lunch. The client loved you! The waiter even loved you! Wait until you tell your boss about the new business rolling in. This is a lunch you'll be able to "hang your hat on" when it comes time for year-end performance reviews.

Standing on the street corner outside the restaurant, you take a deep breath of fresh air. You feel that sense of pride filling your heart like the air filling your lungs. It's another great job done by you. The flashing "Don't Walk" sign across the street tells you to linger on the corner, letting the moment sink in further. A city bus cruises by and you can't help but read the advertisement on the side of the bus. Only it's not an advertisement this time, it's your word jumble. You pull out your BlackBerry and scribble down the letters:

ESE ETH LRAE MHI _____

This word jumble is all about seeing the truth. Soon you're going to be meeting so many great guys that your calendar will be overflowing with dates. For a while, you'll be excited and motivated to meet so many new and interesting people. But going on the dates is only the first part of the equation. It's much more important to know yourself well enough to assess each person against your Wishin' Statement and Souls and Objectives. Remember, every day you spend with the wrong guy is another lost day looking for the right guy.

This chapter is about learning to manage all these terrific men that will start coming into your life. In baseball, managers always say you can never have too many good pitchers. Well, the same holds true in dating. You can never have too many good guys to date. Within that batch of good guys is the great one, and that's what learning to Manage-Men is all about!

## People Management

From: your.boss@work.com
To: you@work.com
Subject: Employee Orientation
On my way 2 a meting. I want u to help orient our neww employee.
Tanks for making it happen.

Before we talk about great men, let's start with great employees. In the last chapter we talked about recruitment and selection as a means to find the ideal candidate for a job. But what happens when the offer is given and accepted? Your work as a manager does not stop there. In fact it's only just beginning. Now your focus shifts from convincing the employees to join your organization to setting them up for success once they've come onboard. With all the costs and time spent finding new employees, there's a lot at stake in giving them the tools and resources he or she needs to hit the ground running when they join the company. It's called effective management, which leads us right into our business definition for this chapter.

> **JEFF'S DEF•I•NI•TIONS:** According to the Society for Human Resource Management, performance management is the process of maintaining or improving employee job performance through the use of performance assessment tools, coaching, and counseling as well as providing continuous feedback.

### The First 100 Days in Office

Think back to any recent presidential election. From the moment a new president takes his oath, his attention turns to the first 100 days in office. This time period, approximately three months, represents a president's efforts to make a big impact right from the start. They want to show some positive results and build momentum for the remainder of their time in office. As a manager of people, particularly newly hired employees, you should take the same approach. The more early victories you can guide your new employees toward, the more momentum they'll generate to contribute to the organization in the long term.

### Management in Action

So let's pretend you just hired a new employee. What are the steps you would actually take to set him or her up for success? Have no fear—once we cover management from a business perspective, we'll jump to dating and figure out the steps you would take to set up a new relationship for success.

1. **Basic orientation:** You may have been at the company for years, but everything is brand new for your new employee, from the 401(k) plan to the meeting schedule to the location

of the bathrooms. So, first things first, you would want to cover all the basics for your newbie, including the job description, benefits, introductions to colleagues, etc.

2. **Talent inventory:** While you would celebrate the success of hiring this employee, recruitment and selection does not stop there. You want a pool of great candidates ready for future openings that may arise in the business. So you would keep the recruitment channels and networks you've worked hard to put into place, all just in case there are openings down the road.

3. **Initial assessment:** As your new employee starts diving into projects and assignments, you would likely complete an initial assessment to see how he or she was doing against the goals established from day one.

4. **Recognition and coaching:** Based on your assessment, you would want to reward and recognize positive behaviors and results. Even a simple thank you or "You're doing a great job" would communicate a positive vibe to your new employee. On the flip side, if you're noticing behaviors that need to be changed, modified, or improved, you would start giving feedback to the employee to help build on these improvement areas.

### Meet Debra, Your Newest Employee

Let's bring these four steps to life. Pretend you just hired Debra to be a new marketing analyst at your company. Debra will be one of your direct reports, and today is her first day. Here's how you might maneuver through these four steps as Debra's leader:

1. **Basic orientation:** There's plenty you could do to welcome Debra. You might start with a welcome lunch to introduce Debra to her colleagues, followed by a tour of the office. Next, you might cover her basic responsibilities through a job description or goal setting. Finally, you would acclimate Debra to her first few assignments and get her started in her new role.

2. **Talent inventory:** Thanks to all your fantastic recruiting efforts, you now have a wide network of headhunters, personal contacts, and Web sites to act as a pipeline of great talent.

While you fully expect Debra to become a high performer, there's no reason to cut off this great network. You want to keep this pipeline in place, especially if another job opens up in your company down the road. So you make it a point to regularly stay connected to this network.

3. **Initial assessment:** After a few weeks on the job, you'll want to take a step back and assess Debra's performance. This is not a formal performance review, rather a brief check-in. What's she doing well? What areas need improvement? How can you help her make a bigger impact on the job? You could package this all up into a brief report to share with Debra. Or you could take her out for an informal lunch to discuss what's going well versus not so well in these early days on the job.

4. **Recognition and coaching:** The assessment would need to be more than lip service. If Debra jumped right into a new product launch and really made an impact, you'd reward her for that. It might be a gift card or small bonus, or even a simple thank-you note depending on the guidelines at your company. On the flip side, if she's missing the mark on some assignments, you would find the right way to offer this constructive feedback. Hopefully these development areas would show rapid improvement after your expert coaching and feedback.

## Let's Start Mixing Business with Pleasure— Dating Pleasure, That Is!

From: your.boss@work.com
To: you@work.com
Subject: Dating Orientation
On my way 2 a meting. I want u to help orient dis new guy ur dating.
Tanks for making it happen.

Successfully onboarding a new employee is a lot like starting a new relationship. Okay, it's not exactly like starting a new relationship, since you can't lead your new man the exact same way you would lead Debra.

However, you can apply the same concepts to helping lead this man in getting your relationship off to a great start. Of course, you might think this whole process would be easier if the guy reported to you, but . . . let's not go there.

---

## Corporate Memo

TO: All Employees
FROM: Carol Cohen
RE: Your Love Life

---

Before Jeff jumps into the four management steps as applied to dating, I want to raise an important business concept: conflict of interest. You're probably familiar with this term in the business setting. This is a situation where you have competing commitments that interfere with your ability to objectively perform your responsibilities. As high-performing, successful women, we would never let a conflict of interest get in the way of our performance. We would be open and honest with ourselves about the situation and rectify the conflicts to continue moving forward.

One of the biggest conflicts of interest in dating is . . . *the dreaded Ex.* Sometimes, even when we know our relationship with an Ex is over, for some reason our thoughts drift back to them, even while we're on dates with new and interesting men. I don't have to tell you how competing thoughts about two guys can wreck your chances with both of them. First of all, you're likely not getting back together with your ex-boyfriend. Second, the new guy will likely pick up on your lingering thoughts about the ex. And what a turn-off that will be! So before you even jump into managing men as Jeff is about to describe, ask yourself whether or not you have any *Dating Conflicts of Interest.* If you don't, that's great and you can move forward. If you do, now's the time to face *the Ex* head-on, create the closure you need, and clear your mind to let in a new, great guy.

---

**JEFF'S DEF•I•NI•TIONS:** According to *Dating, Inc.*, Manage-Men is the process of maintaining or improving relationship performance by your guy through the use of dating assessment tools, coaching, and counseling, as well as providing continuous (okay, how about intermittent) feedback.

# First Date Jitters

It's only natural to feel anxiety before a first date. After all, you're a Super-Star at work, but I'll bet you still feel anxious before a big presentation in front of a new client or your first day in a new job. Remember, anxiety doesn't mean you're going to bomb the first date—it just means you're anxious to jump into action. So what does it take to nail that all-important first date? We decided to go straight to the source and asked three successful, single women in our SuperStar Network for their best first date tips.

### Sally, 44, Insurance Agent from Baltimore, Maryland, on the Do's and Don'ts of First Dates

"Do be yourself and carry yourself in a respectful manner. Show the initiative and willingness to find out more about the other person. Do give yourself time to feel people out before developing any precon-ceptions about them. *Don't* come across as too opinionated until you have developed a certain rapport with the other person. Avoid coming across as a know-it-all. Been there, done that attitudes are simply not attractive and rarely show people in a good light."

### Ashley, 31, Lawyer from Auckland, New Zealand, on the Legal Side of Dating

"From my legal background as a trial lawyer, the most important concept I incorporated into my dating life was the discovery phase. In the beginning of a lawsuit the parties take part in a discovery process where they are required to exchange important and relevant informa-tion so both sides can proceed on equal footing in the case. While dating, the individuals hopefully take part in a similar process so they know relevant information about each other, where they stand, and whether it is worthwhile to proceed with the relationship."

### Kimberly, 52, Wedding Planner from St. Paul, Minnesota, on the Importance of Ice Breakers

"If there is one thing everyone has in common, it's the comfort found in good food and drink. Food is a key part of most of our lives. It's a centerpiece for holiday functions, and what brings families and friends together all around the world. In the business world, food is a way of bringing a little happiness into the daily grind. Working lunches or dinners always feel more fun and are often seen as rewards. These meetings usually promise a higher energy level. This is probably why most first dates occur at a restaurant or over snacks/soda at a movie theater. Dining out is an easy way to feel entertained while on a first date. There is a sense of comfort knowing you're doing something together."

## Corporate Memo

TO: All Employees
FROM: Carol Cohen
RE: Your Love Life

Sally, Ashley, and Kimberly offer great first date advice and tips. To me, the most important thing is to keep your Wishin' Statement and Souls and Objectives front and center when you go on first dates. Think about it. Would you ever ignore your mission statement and goals at work while cranking away on an important project? Of course not! Working hard on a project without considering your long-term mission and goals is a one-way ticket to wasting your time. We know this so clearly at work, so why not keep this thought top of mind on first dates, too? Be honest with yourself. If the guy is the furthest thing from your Wishin' Statement and Souls and Objectives, then you cut bait and move on to the next lucky guy. The more we can stop tricking ourselves into believing any man can be what we're looking for, the more we can focus on the pursuit of a great man who really does meet the criteria we're looking for in a partner. Or if he does meet the criteria from your Wishin' Statement and Souls and Objectives, but falls short after the first date, don't be afraid to admit it's not working and move on.

## First Date Quiz Time

I would never leave you hanging out there on your own when it comes to assessing a man on the first date. So here's a nine-question quiz to help you figure out if he is worthy of a second date, and beyond. I don't recommend taking this quiz in front of him, but definitely give it a try right when you get home. It's the surest way to tell if your guy is even in the ballpark of someone worthy of another date. Read each question, and then circle the answer that best describes how you feel.

Question #1:

**If you compare this man to your Wishin' Statement, he**

    a.   Sounds exactly like the man I described

    b.   Could be the man I described with some minor modifications

    c.   Is probably allergic to the man described in my Wishin' Statement

Question #2:

**If you think about the personality traits he's shown so far, he**

    a.   Possesses many of the must-have qualities I'm seeking

    b.   Falls mostly into my nice-to-have qualities

    c.   Shows mostly traits that are on my who-cares list

Question #3:

**When I look at him only for his looks**

    a.   My heart goes pitter-patter

    b.   I could learn to find him attractive

    c.   I'd rather not look at him if I don't have to

Question #4:

**When I think about the conversation flow at our first date**

    a.   We were finishing each other's sentences

    b.   The conversation was good, with a few awkward silences

    c.   We each spent the whole date talking on our cell phones

## Question #5:
**If I had to introduce him to my family today**
    a.    I would be proud to have him on my arm
    b.    He wouldn't blow them away, but they'd approve
    c.    I really hope my parents are out of town this week

## Question #6:
**If my best friend were on the date with us, he or she would say**
    a.    Don't let this one get away
    b.    Give him a chance, you may grow to like him
    c.    Let's get away fast

## Question #7:
**When I picture any form of intimacy with him**
    a.    I can't wait to feel his lips against mine
    b.    I'll make that call after we're intimate for the first time
    c.    I feel a little sick in my stomach

## Question #8:
**If he were to call me and ask me out for a second date**
    a.    I'd say yes right away
    b.    I'd probably say yes, but wouldn't be super excited
    c.    I'd make an excuse to not go out with him again

## Question #9:
**If this man someday became my husband**
    a.    I'd be honored to stand by his side
    b.    Too early to tell how I'd feel
    c.    We'd be headed for divorce

Now go back and review your answers. For every "a" you circled, award yourself three points, for every "b" you get two points, and for every "c" circled, give yourself one point. Add all the points together to get a final score. So what does it all mean?

- **If you scored between 19 and 27 points:** This guy is pretty darn close to your Wishin' Statement and Souls and Objectives. If you haven't already agreed to a second date, by all means, call him up! Be sure this is in your plans. You seem to have found a great guy, so definitely keep the dates coming with him to see where it goes.

- **If you scored between 10 and 18 points:** You have a case of a "middle of the road guy" on your hands. He probably has some traits you really desire in a partner, and others you could do without. Ask yourself this bonus question: Are you someone who has a history of being overly picky? If the answer is "yes," then give this guy another shot. Go on a couple more dates, take the quiz again in a few weeks, and see if your score goes up or down.

- **If you scored between 1 and 9 points:** Please tell me you've already canceled this guy out. If you've moved on to the next guy, then you've done a great job of realizing quickly that this guy does not match your Wishin' Statement and Souls and Objectives. If you are planning to date this guy again, then ask yourself this bonus question: Why are you investing more time in someone who possesses very little of what you're looking for in a man?

### Don't Settle for Less When You Can Settle for More

No, I am not advocating dating twenty guys at once. However, remember that at this phase, we're not talking about monogamy yet. That means there's no reason to turn down first dates while you're going on second and third dates with other men. Until you find that special someone worthy of a monogamous relationship with you, then you want to keep that dating pipeline, or as they say in business, that talent inventory we spoke of earlier, intact.

### Women's Intuition

Eleanor, a vice president of sales in the media industry, believes cold calling is a lot like dating. It's how she keeps a constant influx of potential business prospects in the sales pipeline and how she also keeps a constant influx of potential partners in the dating pipeline. "In the sales world, making cold calls is a fact of life. Most salespeople hate making cold calls because nine times out of ten, they are rejected by the person on the other end of the phone. Once a salesperson has proven himself/herself, their managers will gradually feed them 'warm leads,' to encourage and reward their efforts. A 'warm lead' is something or someone that already has a strong interest in your product or service. In other words, they are predisposed to buy your product because they have heard from a friend/business associate that your product is of high quality.

Warm leads are very helpful to those eager to find Mr. or Mrs. Right. Having a friend set you up or recommend a first meeting is just like a 'warm lead' and makes all the difference in the world. If one agrees to the date, they are actually saying 'Yes, I am interested in welcoming someone into my life.' More importantly, you know the person 'checks out' and they've been given the stamp of approval by your friend(s)."

### Maintain Your Own Dating Pipeline

Okay, it's time to talk odds. Now, I really do hope that, when you master the concepts in this book, you'll run out and meet someone fantastic on your first try. However, the odds are high that despite your best efforts to meet quality men, the first few people you meet may not be quite what you're looking for in a partner. Rather than feel discouraged, I want you to instead focus on keeping a dating pipeline alive and kicking at all times. This means, until you decide on one man for a monogamous relationship, you should keep up your connection to a bunch of great guys at all stages of the dating cycle, including:

- Guys with whom you are in the midst of second and third dates
- Guys you have just gone on first dates with
- Guys you are about to go on first dates with
- Guys you have just met that you are talking to about first dates
- Guys you are trying to meet to potentially have first dates

If you can have all five scenarios going at the same time, you'll have a continuously fresh pipeline of people to choose from. Hopefully one of these guys will emerge from the pack as the one worthy of a monogamous relationship. If not, move him out! And keep moving new men through your dating pipeline until Mr. Right emerges.

---

### Corporate Memo

TO: All Employees
FROM: Carol Cohen
RE: Your Love Life

---

The idea of a dating pipeline reminds me of when I used to work in retail. One of the products we offered through our department stores was women's shoes. Let's apply this concept of a pipeline to the inventory of shoes for our customers. At any given time we had shoes:

- Currently being worn in public by our customers
- Just bought in our stores and about to be worn for the first time
- On display in our stores to be tried on by our customers
- In production by our manufacturers to be shipped to our stores
- In design mode to be offered in the next season

This approach to selling shoes created a constant pipeline of new options for our female customers. There's no reason women can't do the same in dating. If you can have great guys in all the stages of dating, then you have the best possible shot of meeting the right one for you.

❲ So you're thinking a Dating Inventory sounds good in theory. But how do you actually make it happen in your real-life dating scene? Here are three ideas you could do today to keep your Dating Inventory alive and well:

1. Keep your online profile active: If you're participating in online dating, there is no reason to immediately put your membership on hold just because you're casually dating someone. When you decide to become monogamous and have that conversation with your partner, that's the time to cancel a membership or put it on hold.

2. Keep the setups coming: Keep reminding friends, family members, and colleagues that you're open to blind dates and setups. They may see you actively dating and think you no longer need any help meeting a great guy. But you're actually better off if they keep thinking of setups for you. Keep that pipeline flowing until you really are ready to put an end to the influx of potential partners.

3. Commit to new clubs and activities: Find new and interesting ways to meet men you wouldn't otherwise meet. Join a new organization, work out at a new gym, pick up a new sport, anything that gets you in front of a new set of people to find new prospects for dating. ❳

## Assess Before You Digress

If you play it right during these early stages, you really will have a host of guys at each of the early stages of a relationship I described above. But how do you decide which ones have a shot at something long term and which ones should be thrown back in the dating pool?

The answer lies in a simple assessment. At this stage, we're assuming he scored high enough on the first date quiz that he's advanced to second dates and beyond. This would be like a direct report at work that made it through the first couple of months and now it's time to size him up to figure out what kind of employee he'll really be. So how do you complete this assessment when it comes to dating? The answer lies in rewarding what's working and providing coaching on what's falling short.

In a recent Catalyst study about women in leadership, 69 percent of women say they get ahead at work by consistently exceeding expectations, 49 percent by successfully managing others, and 47 percent say they have developed a style with which male managers are comfortable. If you can apply these findings and strategies to your dating life, you can get ahead of the pack in relationships too!

## Thank You for a Job Well Done

I believe in having optimistic views on life and dating, so let's start with the upside. Before you get into things you want to change about a given guy, what is he doing really well? What should he be rewarded for? Does he plan interesting dates? Does he call when he says he'll call? Does he actively listen to you on dates and remember details about your life? Only you know what behaviors make you smile, but it's important to recognize these behaviors and let your guy know you appreciate them.

## Corporate Memo

TO: All Employees
FROM: Carol Cohen
RE: Your Love Life

When you recognize an employee at work for a job well done, have you ever noticed that the person becomes more motivated, more engaged in work, and more likely to produce positive results in the future? Why not apply the same logic to the men you're meeting? If they're showing behaviors that you like, let them know about it. This is the best way to improve your odds of seeing these same behaviors in the future. This puts a clear spotlight on what he should keep doing or even do more often instead of leaving him in the dark.

## Pat 'Em on the Back

So what are the current men in your life doing really well? What deserves some recognition by you? Make that list right now and put pen to paper on where these men are surpassing your expectations.

Guy #1 deserves recognition for _____

_____

Guy #2 deserves recognition for _____

_____

Guy #3 deserves recognition for _____

_____

Once you make this list, don't just keep it to yourself. Tell each of them what makes him special and why he deserves some recognition for his efforts. What's the best way to give this recognition? Simply agree to more dates with the guys who show the most behaviors worthy of recognition—getting to spend lots of time with a fabulous woman like you is reward in and of itself! And be sure to let him know that special something you like about him. By doing that, you'll also keep the right ones in your pipeline!

### There's Good News and Bad News

Okay, so it can't all be a rosy picture, and inevitably there will be some areas that you wish you could you change about your guy. The key here is to be realistic. This is not the time to write down something like, "He really needs to be three inches taller." Instead we're looking for personality tweaks or minor behavior changes that you know would go a long way and make you like him even more. So for each of the men we just wrote nice things about, we're now going to write down areas that could use some improving.

Guy #1 needs coaching and feedback on _____

_____

Guy #1 needs coaching and feedback on _____

_____

Guy #1 needs coaching and feedback on _____

_____

# Easy Does It

So you've got a few things you wish you could fine-tune about the guys you're dating. You're even thinking if one of these guys could make the slight improvement, he could really be monogamous boyfriend material. However, if you just blurt out a bunch of things the guy needs to change, he may get scared off and make his own change—finding someone new to date. The recognition messages were so much easier, but how do you deliver the constructive feedback? The answer lies in thinking about coaching and feedback from a business perspective.

### *The Coach Approach*

So how do you deliver the message and get the results you're looking for? Thomas, a customer service representative from Mexico, believes "There is not one right approach to coaching and feedback. You have to find a way to deliver your message so that the recipient will be as receptive as possible. If they are not open to it, you could tell them the secret of eternal love and happiness and they wouldn't hear it! In the business world, where there is a great diversity of perspectives, it is important to tailor your message to the recipient. With some people you can be very direct, for others your feedback needs to be carefully couched."

Anna, the owner of a small bakery in Milwaukee, Wisconsin, believes in "approaching your partner with empathy and humility. I don't ever try and come off as if I know everything, but if constructive feedback is required, I make sure I have specific examples to back up my feedback, versus using emotion and vague words. I also make sure to always counter constructive feedback with positive feedback. There are always areas where they can be praised. In instances where I am coaching, I think the humility aspect really works well, because nobody wants to listen to a know-it-all, but if you give examples of mistakes you have made in the past that have helped you learn the specific lesson you're trying to convey, it helps to provide empathy to the situation."

Julie, a stay-at-home mom from Cleveland, Ohio, thinks that just like in business, dating coaching "involves clearly communicating what is going well and what is not going well in the relationship and how you can improve the relationship. This doesn't need to be a formal plan but rather the communication around the relationship. You cannot assume that your boyfriend is a mind reader. Therefore, you need to tell him what you like and don't like and how he is not meeting your needs."

## We've Got Our Men Managed

In the end, it's all about assessing, rewarding, and coaching these potential Mr. Rights in the early stages of dating to see which ones have a real shot at moving forward to the monogamous relationship phase. If you can master the skills in this chapter while keeping that pipeline of dating prospects rolling in, you'll soon be ready for Section 3 of this book, The One. This is the point where you're ready to exit the stream of dating prospects and really give it a go with one guy.

## The Bottom Line

You're ready to move on to the next chapter if the following are true:

- You understand the importance of effectively managing people in an organization.
- You can translate the concept of managing people at a company to managing men in the dating world.
- You feel confident you can create a dating pipeline for yourself to keep that influx of great guys coming in at all times.
- You understand how to assess men to arrive at the behaviors that deserve recognition versus those that require coaching and feedback.
- You believe you're ready to learn how to go from dating a variety of men to choosing one standout gentleman for a monogamous relationship.

section

# The One

Okay, I'd love to say that at this point in the book you have found your one true love, your soul mate. You have found the person who finishes your sentences, spoons you tight, and cares for you like nobody else. That would really set up this section nicely! If you have found that person already, then I congratulate you, and ask that you send thank-you letters and wedding invitations directly to me at *contact@datingincbook.com*.

That's not really what this section is all about, though. The reason this section is called "The One" is because at this point you are ready to make an important transition. You're going from dating lots of potential partners and keeping your eyes peeled for dating prospects to narrowing your candidate pool and deciding who is the best of the best. By the end of this stage, you'll give one of the lucky bachelors you have been gracing with your presence a chance at a monogamous relationship. If he turns out to be "The One"—for real and forever—then that's great. I know the savvy businesswoman in you will be able to tell whether the guy you're dating has a chance at developing into something truly long term. Plus, if making that decision scares you a bit, then this section will absolutely help you make that determination about your guy.

Section 3 consists of three chapters designed specifically to keep a fabulous guy around, help you determine if he should stick around long term, and guide you as you begin building a life together. Who knows—at this stage, you might even start entertaining words like "engagement" and "marriage."

In Chapter 7, we'll start with the business principle of customer service. You'll learn why customer service departments do everything they can to keep customers that meet their ideal profile or target market. We'll then apply this business principle to the dating principle of Lust-omer Service. Here you'll learn what it takes to keep a great guy interested before you consider going back to the dating pool to attract a brand-new guy. In this chapter you'll learn how to keep your fantastic man lusting after you from day one of the relationship.

In Chapter 8, we'll cover how companies assess the employee talent in their organization. This is how companies determine which of their employees are the SuperStars, the steady-eddies, and which ones need to ultimately get managed out of the organization. The talent assessment process keeps the high performers moving up in the organization to face bigger challenges while the underachievers are encouraged to change jobs or look for opportunities elsewhere. We'll take this talent assessment process and apply it to the dating scene through a concept called Talent Assess-Men. This is where you'll take a clear step back from your relationship to make sure your guy is performing up to snuff. This assessment of your guy and the state of your relationship will help you decide if it's time to get more serious, slow things down, or even break up and start fresh.

In our joint venture chapter, we'll examine how two companies join forces to pool their resources and tackle the marketplace together. This process, which typically includes months of philosophical discussion and joint goal setting, ensures the combined company is stronger and more efficient than the two companies operating alone. We'll take this business concept and apply it to Dating Principle #9, Joint Adventure. This is the point when a couple really sees a future together and realizes they're a stronger unit together than separate. You've decided that you want to go on that Joint Adventure through life together. This is all about making that ultimate commitment, engagement, marriage, or some kind of life partnership. We won't cover wedding planning in this chapter—there's an entire industry out there devoted to that topic—rather, we'll discuss life planning. We already know couples spend months planning every last detail of their wedding together. That event is usually four hours or less. What about the rest of your lives together? Here you'll learn what it takes to complete a relationship philosophy, the guiding principles for couples who want to merge their lives together with the least amount of disruption and make their relationships work. You'll learn how to develop a short- and long-term relationship plan and get on the road to achieving your joint dreams as a couple.

---

### Corporate Memo

TO: All Employees
FROM: Carol Cohen
RE: Your Love Life

---

I know we're taught from the moment we're little girls to think of engagement and marriage as the classic fairy-tale ending. But how many of your friends actually describe the experience this way? Well, you don't just live happily ever after just because you said "I do!" We know it takes a lot of work to put together a wedding with lasting memories, and it takes even more work to make a relationship last! The same holds true in business. Our best working relationships are built over time through mutual respect and honesty. When we're clicking with someone at work, we actually look forward to partnering on projects together. But this chemistry doesn't happen overnight. It takes months, sometimes years to find the right balance! Relationships are similar in that respect. We want it to be easy, but we know that the comfort level only comes after putting in the work to build a strong relationship. So while it's okay to dream about our weddings, let's also remember how much work we put into building strong relationships at the office. That same approach can help us build long-lasting relationships in the romance department.

---

## The One or Time to Run?

Let's get to work now on Section 3. By the time we're through, you'll know for sure whether the great guy you found truly deserves a piece of your heart or his walking papers. Let's get started!

# chapter **seven**

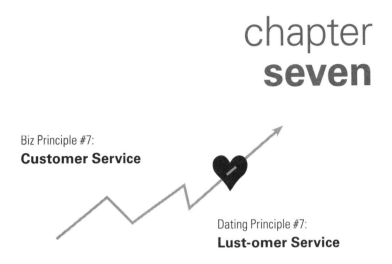

## Agenda

- The importance of customer service in keeping quality clients
- How retention plans keep high-performing employees onboard
- How a retention plan can keep great guys in a relationship
- The best ways to introduce intimacy into a relationship

## Work/Life Balance

There's nothing like that feeling of riding high after an important business meeting that goes well. You feel like you can conquer the world. Back at your desk after debriefing with your boss on the lunch meeting, you're still smiling ear to ear. This is not an arrogant thing, just an inner confidence for a job well done. You spend the next two and a half hours catching up from the morning, answering e-mails, returning phone calls, checking in with colleagues and direct reports. It's back to the typical day for you.

By 3:30 P.M. your fingers are feeling tired from all the typing and your ear needs a break from conference calls. You're also feeling that mid-afternoon twinge of hunger. You suddenly remember that protein bar in your briefcase. That should really hit the spot. Reaching in to your bag to pull out the snack, you come across today's newspaper. You forgot you had tucked it into your briefcase just before arriving at work. With your right hand you continue digging for the protein bar, but your eyes can't help but catch the words on the paper. Wouldn't you know it, another word jumble is staring right back at you:

AEMK MHI TSLU FRETA UYO _____

After you figure out this word jumble, you'll know what this chapter is all about. I know at work you do your best to control your own destiny. That's what makes you a SuperStar on the job. You don't leave things to chance. You do everything in your power to get the job done and keep your customers and colleagues smiling. Why not take the same approach in your relationship? If you have a great guy in your arms, you can take control of the relationship. This does not mean dominating or controlling your guy. It just means doing everything in your power to give the relationship the best shot at survival. If you decide it's time to walk away, let it be your decision or one you make together. By mastering the tools in this chapter, you can say goodbye to great guys walking away from you when you're not ready to end the relationship.

## First a Word on Customer Service

From: your.boss@work.com
To: you@work.com
Subject: Retention Plan
We have 2 keep our grate new hirre onboard.
Make a plan 2 keep em around and tree tem like a customer.
Tanks for making it happen.

Whether companies want to keep their best customers or employees on board, quality retention plans are key. It's so much easier to retain a great customer or employee than start over prospecting for new ones.

This is why companies invest so much money in creating and maintaining robust retention plans.

Let's start with a look at customer service and how it relates to retaining quality customers. There's no better place to start than the definition of customer service.

> **JEFF'S DEF•I•NI•TIONS:** According to Wikipedia, customer service is the set of behaviors that a business undertakes during its interaction with its customers.

With all the super-savvy businesswomen we've been interviewing for this book, we realized we had the perfect people to ask about what it takes to achieve best-in-class customer service levels. Here's a compilation of the top ten ways companies can satisfy their customers:

1. Bring positive results for the customer and contribute to their bottom line.
2. Master the "what's in it for me" perspective, or WIIFM. In other words, master thinking from the customer's point of view.
3. Build trust with customers and exceed their expectations.
4. Treat customers with a personal touch to make them feel valued.
5. Consistently deliver a quality product and service.
6. Pay close attention to the specific needs and desires of each customer so they feel unique and special.
7. Be responsive to customers when things go wrong to resolve any and all complaints and issues.
8. Be open to customer suggestions and feedback to improve the products and services offered in the future.
9. Keep a close eye on the competitors to make sure your customers always feel you deliver a better product or service than they could get elsewhere.
10. Communicate regularly with customers through multiple channels to personalize the relationship and keep your company top of mind.

Put it all together and it seems the key to quality customer service is honesty, responsiveness, openness, communication, and listening. Do these sound important in relationships, too? If you said yes, you are absolutely right! But don't get ahead of us—we'll shift to dating and relationships in a moment. Not surprisingly, when we asked our savvy businesswomen and businessmen for the quickest way to ruin a customer relationship, they indicated it comes down to violating any of the items on the top-ten list. We heard quotes like these:

- "A company can really mess up with customers, but as long as they adhere to the basics of good customer service, people tend to be very forgiving, and they are generally willing to give the company another chance. If companies ignore the rules of good customer service, clients go elsewhere in a hurry."—James, 41, financial analyst
- "Companies can easily lose loyal customers if they take them for granted or display actions that erode the relative importance of that client. Customers may also jump ship if the company is outdone by an aggressive competitor who makes concerted efforts to step up and gain that customer's business."—Leslie, 33, marketing executive

---

## Corporate Memo

TO: All Employees
FROM: Carol Cohen
RE: Your Love Life

---

When we're at work, we know how to keep good clients around. We'll do whatever it takes to keep them happy. This does not make us a doormat or a push-over; it just means we value the upside of the client (that is, profitability) over the downside (difficulty in dealing with the customer). There's no reason we can't apply this same logic to retaining a great guy. If you know in your heart that there's more upside (you love him) than downside (he goes out with the boys too much), then you can work through the downside to keep the great guy in the relationship. That's what good customer service is all about, and the same applies in dating and relationships.

### *Retention from the Employee Perspective*

Retention of great customers is not the only thing that matters for a company to be successful. The best and brightest employees need to be motivated and engaged in their work. Otherwise the products, services, and ultimately customers will suffer.

To find out what it takes to achieve superior employee retention, we went back to our savvy businesswomen and asked them. Here's another top-ten list, this time focused on the best ways to keep a motivated work force:

## Top Ten Talent Motivation Tips

1. Offer employees rewards (i.e., bonuses) for a job well done.
2. Create an environment where employees feel challenged by their assignments.
3. Continuously say thank you and provide other means of recognition when employees get the job done.
4. Strive to maintain a work atmosphere that fosters teamwork and collaboration.
5. Listen to employee suggestions in order to improve their work satisfaction.
6. Understand the need for work/life balance and allow employees the space to deal with personal needs.
7. Promote high-performing employees to continuously stretch them and allow them to grow into their next roles.
8. Offer mentors and coaches in the organization to guide employees in their personal development.
9. Maintain a people leadership model that builds trust and teamwork among employees.
10. Actively listen to employee needs and act like an advocate.

Just as we summed up the top-ten list on the customer service side, let's look at the themes from the employee perspective. It seems that employee retention depends on motivation, rewards, challenges, communication, and guidance. Now go back to the list again and realize just how many of those nifty notions can apply to your dating life! So keep those words in mind—we'll revisit these themes when we switch to dating and relationships in a moment.

### Women's Intuition

With all these fantastic female business leaders at our fingertips, we couldn't help but ask what it takes to lead and motivate a workforce. Cassandra, a talented sales executive from London, England, offered this advice for work and relationships:

"You can't expect a talented employee to be good at everything. For example, the top salesperson may not be the best with paperwork on the back end. Or the best accountant may not be able to make a presentation in front of a large group. Likewise in relationships, you can't expect your partner to fulfill all of your needs. There may be certain activities he doesn't like to do or topics he doesn't like to discuss. You may need to look to a girlfriend or a family member for fulfillment in a couple areas. When it comes to retaining a great employee, you have to grow them, challenge them, compliment them often, and let them know they are appreciated. Your competitor is always trying to recruit your employees and headhunters are always on the prowl. If you take the time to communicate regularly with your employees by creating an open door policy, encouraging honest candor and showing respect, they will be less likely to accept offers from others. The same holds true for relationships."

## Now How Do You Retain a Great Guy?

From: your.boss@work.com
To: you@work.com
Subject: Employee Retention
We have 2 keep dis grate new guy in da relationship.
Make a plan 2 keep em around.
Tanks for making it happen.

Let's take what we just learned about customer and employee retention and apply it to keeping that great guy around. Remember, we're not yet talking about keeping him around forever. We're just saying that if the relationship is off to a good start, there are definite steps you can take to keep both of you interested in the relationship, while you decide on Mr. Right-Now's long-term potential.

Let's start by converting our customer service definition to dating and relationships.

> **JEFF'S DEF•I•NI•TIONS:** According to *Dating, Inc.*, Lust-omer Service is the set of behaviors that a savvy, successful woman undertakes during her interactions with a great guy.

## Twenty Words That Make All the Difference

Let's revisit the two top-ten lists from the customer and employee sections and pull the most important word from each item on the list. Here's what we come up with:

- Positive
- Trust
- Quality
- Responsive
- Deliver
- Rewards
- Thanks
- Listen
- Grow
- Teamwork

- What's in it for me (WIIFM)
- Valued
- Needs
- Open
- Communicate
- Challenge
- Satisfaction
- Understand
- Coach
- Advocate

Wow, just look at that list! Imagine if you met someone who embodied most or all of these words. Look at that list again. Doesn't it just make you smile to think about a person who lives by these words? Guess what? If these words are powerful enough to keep great customers on board and great employees at the office, then they certainly can keep a great guy in a relationship.

**action item**

{ I'll bet you already portray more than a few words on the top-twenty list above. Now is your chance to add to your repertoire. At work, you're always trying to learn new skills, so let's apply that philosophy to dating. Pick a few words from the list that you *know* you don't currently live by as well as you could in your relationships. We're going to make the conscious decision to flip your mindset on these words, and incorporate them into your dating style. For example:

> **Words you don't live by:** You don't currently make a habit of saying thank you for nice things your guy does.
>
> **How to live by it:** Start a Thank-You Campaign. Simply say it or even write it in a love note when your man cooks a delicious meal, surprises you with a weekend getaway, or gives you a sensuous thirty-minute massage after a long day at the office.
>
> **Words you don't live by:** You have been slow to open up to your man in previous relationships.
>
> **How to live by it:** Take a shot at showing more trust early on. Share some of those embarrassing stories from your childhood, open up about a few of your fears. I'll bet the anxiety of opening up will quickly be replaced by comfort and love from an understanding guy.
>
> **Words you don't live by:** You are the one who tends to think WIIFM (what's in it for me) at the beginning of the relationship.
>
> **How to live by it:** Keep the acronym, but think about it from your guy's perspective. Why should he be in a relationship with you? What do you have to offer that he can't find with someone else? Play up those differentiators with your man to make him see just how lucky he is to have you around. }

## So What Will You Commit To?

You've seen the top-twenty list, and you've read a few examples. Now what can you apply right here, right now to your relationship? This is your chance to commit to adding three new retention strategies to keep your great guy interested. Using the twenty words as guidance, write three retention statements here. (What's that you say? You still need an example? How about "I will remember to thank my man for dropping me off every day for work, even though it's twenty miles out of the way for him"):

Retention Statement #1 _____

_____

Retention Statement #2 _____

_____

Retention Statement #3 _____

_____

---

### Corporate Memo

TO: All Employees
FROM: Carol Cohen
RE: Your Love Life

---

Think about all the areas of our lives where we proactively control our destiny. At work, eating habits, working out, budgeting—the list goes on and on. There are so many ways we guide our lives. But for some reason, when it comes to relationships, sometimes we feel helpless. Where is that inner compass that so deftly guides us through all the other aspects of our lives? For some reason, the emotional roller coaster of relationships feels like too much to handle. To me, that's where a retention strategy makes a lot of sense. It's our opportunity to control our relationship destinies. Sure, it's not a guarantee that the relationship will work out with your someone special *du moment.* But it does give us the best shot of keeping the romance alive while we figure out just how long we want a particular person in our lives. So take advantage of what you know at work about retaining great customers and employees—it will pay huge dividends in your dating life too!

---

## A Word About Bediquette

When you talk about a relationship getting more serious, you can't help but talk about intimacy. We could of course write a whole book on this subject alone, but in this case, we got really lucky. One of the super-savvy businesswomen we interviewed just happens to be a sex expert. Her name is Christy Rosen, and here's what she had to say about intimacy in relationships:

"Low or poor self-esteem is the root of all evil in intimate relationships. If you feel bad about yourself, whether it's about your physical appearance, your sexual experience (or lack of), insecurity about your relationship, or any of the myriad other things there are to be down on yourself about, it can affect your ability to experience and enjoy an intimate relationship. Really, the key to enjoying intimacy is being comfortable with yourself and trusting your partner enough to know that whatever happens between the two of you is okay. I still remember an incident with one of my first 'real' boyfriends—we were in the middle of 'things' when I fell off the bed. Now to some people this would have been a horrifyingly embarrassing situation; to me, it was insanely hysterical and the two of us could not stop laughing.

Taking oneself too seriously in the bedroom can be very damaging. Things happen that you don't expect, things go wrong, and this is all very normal. Having the confidence to be flexible (not as in being able to wrap your feet around your head, but the ability to go with the flow and not have too many expectations) and having a sense of humor about it all can really enhance your sexual experience and intimacy with your partner. You don't have to be sexually experienced or look like Angelina Jolie to have a good time with your partner. The silliness of sex (and everyday life, for that matter) can only bring you closer."

While we had our sex expert's ear, we just couldn't help asking her a follow-up question. So we asked Christy what a couple should do if one partner is really adventurous between the sheets, but the other partner is more conservative. Here's her advice if you're struggling with the same issue in your own relationship:

"Everyone has an adventure comfort zone. One partner may consider this to mean wearing sexy lingerie to bed, whereas the other partner thinks this means incorporating whips and chains. I think it's possible for all couples to find a happy medium of comfort and excitement. It's just the nature of things that when you first start dating someone (that you like and he/she likes you back) a lot more experimentation goes on in the bedroom. That isn't to say that experimentation doesn't continue to happen throughout the lifetime of an intimate relationship. The key to finding a happy medium is communication. It's never okay to cajole or bargain with your partner to get them to do something they are not comfortable doing. But it is okay to communicate your feelings, fantasies, and desires."

## ····state of the business #7 ··············

Nearly 16 percent of corporate officers in Fortune 500 companies are women, up from 12.5 percent in 2000. Women are taking on increasingly more senior roles in business. Now's the time to take a stronger role in relationships by applying that same go-getter attitude to your dating approach.

## This Isn't a Sex Book! Back to Retention

We've talked about the steps a woman can take to keep a great guy interested. But what about the flip side of the story? Are there things a woman does or says that are sure to drive a great guy away?

### Why Do Great Guys End Relationships with Great Women?

We interviewed a host of successful businesswomen for this book, but we didn't want to leave the other gender out completely. This question was a perfect opportunity to hear the guy's point of view. So we posed this very question to some successful businessmen to find out if there are specific things a woman does, particular ways a woman acts, that makes him want to walk away from an otherwise great relationship. Here are the top ten findings from our interviews with the guys:

#### Top Ten Turnoffs That Make a Good Guy Wave Goodbye

1. Taking out frustrations from a previous relationship on your current boyfriend.
2. Playing games and acting interested one day, aloof the next.
3. Forcing "the talk" too soon in the relationship, and putting way too much unnecessary pressure on the relationship.

4. Constant prying or snooping that indicates a lack of trust from the beginning.
5. Low self-confidence or self-esteem that translates into a dependence upon the boyfriend to give them a sense of purpose or meaning.
6. Materialism! A shallow obsession with things like cars, money, jewelry, and expensive clothing.
7. Leaving no space for guy time, and thinking that objections to this means a guy doesn't care about the relationship.
8. Emotional ups and downs that leave a guy wondering what version of the girlfriend he'll have on any given day.
9. Insecurity and petty jealousy: when women think any time a guy makes eye contact with another woman he wants to sleep with her.
10. Asking those impossible-to-answer questions, like "Do I look fat," where any answer a guy gives will lead to trouble.

### The Female Perspective

So that's what the guys say can drive them away from a relationship. But what do the women have to say? We asked three of our successful female executives to tell us the worst mistake they ever made in a relationship.

### Evelyn, 31, Nutritionist from Detroit

"The biggest mistake I made in a relationship was staying in one particular relationship way too long and hoping that things would get better. I thought I really loved the person and I thought that the person really loved me. So I put up with a lot of things that I should never have put up with. If I had another chance, I would have dumped him earlier in the relationship and not wasted precious time trying to make things work when I knew it was never going to work. However, this really helped me in my next relationship. When I thought he was jerking me around and wasn't serious about making a commitment, I broke up with him. Two weeks later, we were shopping for an engagement ring."

### Ashley, 43, Writer from New Orleans

"I did not allow myself to see that the other person had very strong feelings for me. I was in denial and could have prevented hurt feelings if I had accepted the fact that he had stronger feelings for me than I had for him. This would have allowed us to be open and honest about where we were with our feelings. I would like to have had the chance to really talk with him about it and discuss things honestly, rather than me just ignoring it and acting like we could be friends."

### Brenda, 51, Management Consultant from San Diego, California

"Letting it go on too long. Just like at work when you have hired someone who is not performing well early on, you should fire them immediately and not go down the road thinking the person is going to miraculously change. If they are not the right fit in dating, get out of the relationship ASAP! Also, when you are just starting out on the dating circuit—date multiple people. There is no reason why you should take a one-at-a-time philosophy. I think early on, I felt like it would be wrong to set up other dates while I just started seeing someone else. This is a numbers game, and you need to meet as many people as possible. You'll know when it's time to go "exclusive.""

## Corporate Memo

TO: All Employees
FROM: Carol Cohen
RE: Your Love Life

If there's one great reminder to take away from the male perspective versus female perspective on why relationships end, it's that there's always two sides to every breakup. It's really the same at the office. When a partnership, sale, or working relationship falters, both sides are quick to blame the other side for the meltdown. But there's also a part of us, even if we don't admit it right away, that knows we need to take responsibility for our part in a failed relationship. To me, that's about the essence of this chapter. If you have a fabulous dreamboat man with you, and you want to see if it has a chance of working out, then you do everything you can to retain him. This is not about tricking him or playing games, it's about applying the skills to our romantic relationships that we know from work keep customers and employees happy. That's the secret to giving it a shot with a terrific man—treat him as well as you would your work associates and colleagues.

## The Bottom Line

In the end it's clear that a great retention plan at work can keep employees happy and motivated on the job. They can also do the same for keeping a great guy interested. So get started on your retention plan today, and your guy will be truly engaged in the relationship. Did somebody say engaged? Let's not get ahead of ourselves!

You're ready to move on to the next chapter if the following are true:

- You understand why companies put in place customer retention programs.
- You know the value of employee retention plans in keeping people motivated.
- You see how customer and employee retention plans apply to keeping a great guy interested.
- You have determined some personal retention tips you'll implement in your own relationship to give it the best shot of working out for the foreseeable future.

# chapter
# **eight**

Biz Principle #8:
**Talent Assessment**

Dating Principle #8:
**Talent Assess-Men**

## Agenda

- How performance reviews help corporations measure employee performance
- How talent assessments help companies measure the performance and potential of their people
- How performance reviews and talent assessments can be applied to the men you are dating
- How to decide to promote, develop, or manage out the guy you're dating

## Work/Life Balance

What a day! It's mid-afternoon, and you are cruising through your work. Cutting deals, answering e-mails, just plain getting things done. Nothing out of the ordinary for a SuperStar like you. Leaning back in your chair, you feel that sense of accomplishment for a job well done. You also feel a small twinge of sleepiness. You decide to take a quick walk to the lobby for a chance to stretch your legs. As you walk around, you can't help but notice a flyer taped to the side of the vending machine. It's a word jumble, imagine that! You immediately set to work on unscrambling the jumble:

VOLE MHI RO EEAVL HMI _____

As you'll see from this word jumble and this chapter, we're about to move into decision-making. Up to this point, we've been talking about landing and keeping a great guy. But at some point along the way you have to decide whether or not the guy you're with is worthy of a longer-term investment or should be shown the door. That's what this word jumble is all about, and that's what we'll be covering to in this chapter. Welcome to Talent Assess-Men!

## What's the Deal with Talent Assessment?

```
From: your.boss@work.com
To: you@work.com
Subject: Talent Assessment
We got 2 rate our employeez on their per4mance
andd potential. Can u set it up?
Tanks for making it happen.
```

If you've ever worked at a corporation or held a position in management, you're probably familiar with the concept of talent management. It's a means for companies to step back from accomplishing goals and review the performance of the employees responsible for making the goals happen. Whether companies are looking at one-year performance or employee potential for the future, the idea is to determine which employees are the high performers, which are the steady eddies, and which ones should be headed toward performance counseling and possibly even the dreaded pink slip. In a moment, we'll apply these same principles to evaluating the guy you're dating. But first, let's make sure we have a good handle on the business concepts. What better place to start than the basic definition of talent assessment?

## The Three Sides of Talent Assessment

Companies group all kinds of processes and procedures under the broad category of talent assessment. Most will at a minimum include at least these three parts:

1. Performance reviews
2. Career potential analysis
3. Coaching and counseling

## Corporate Memo

TO: All Employees
FROM: Carol Cohen
RE: Your Love Life

If you haven't worked in a traditional corporate job, these terms may be foreign to you. So let me just break it down in laywoman's terms for a moment. Pretend you started a company and hired one employee to work for you. After a year together, you'd likely take out some time to reflect on her performance. This could be through a formal performance review or just an informal lunch to give some feedback on the employee's performance in the past year. Over time, you'd think beyond this person's yearly performance and consider whether or not she has a shot at working with you for years to come. In essence, you're not just looking at her most recent performance but expanding your assessment to her long-term potential. That is called a career potential analysis. Finally, once you know how she's doing on a yearly basis and determine her long-term potential, it's decision time. If your employee is a high performer, you coach her to maintain that all-star performance. If she has potential but hasn't reached it yet, you might design a plan to bring out the best in her. If you get the sense she'll never cut it at your company, then you'd figure out a way to get her out of the picture and look to hire a new employee.

### How About an Illustration for a Solid Foundation?

To illustrate the three aspects of talent assessment, let's invent a fictional company together. Let's see how we might incorporate performance reviews, career potential analysis, and coaching/counseling into how we manage our company together. Do you remember our widget discussion from the market plan/Spark-It Plan chapter? Let's make our company the world's leading provider of widgets. Let's also assume that our company employs a hundred people in various roles to manufacture, sell, and deliver our beloved widgets into the hands of our customers. So how might the three aspects of talent assessment play out for our widget company?

1. **Performance reviews:** Every year, in November, we write performance reviews on every employee in the organization. We look at achievements against goals (for instance, how many innovative projects did Joel set out to accomplish last year? Did he attain his goal?), employee strengths (Joel is an incredible communicator about the importance of widgets in the global economy), and development areas (Joel needs to be better about completing his widget paperwork as each project draws to a close).

   All of this rolls together into a rating for each employee. Those ratings help determine raises, bonuses, and promotions. In essence, performance reviews become the means for us to compare the yearly performance of all the employees who played a role in running our widget company. Believe me, manufacturing widgets for a living is no easy task, so there are a lot of employees to review. Some were born to make widgets, while others can't get the hang of it. They fidget with the widget, but never finish manufacturing one!

2. **Career potential analysis:** We want to look at yearly performance but it's also important to consider our employees from a long-term potential perspective (can Joel make a career out of widget production, or was this just one good year?). So we sit in a room and think not just about the current performance of our employees but also the long-term value, or potential,

for each employee. We might even graph performance versus potential for our employees, looking for those who show the strongest performance and highest potential. As leaders of our widget company, we need to find the people who can produce widgets like nobody's business—the real widget wizards who crank these things out faster than a dog chasing a bone. These employees become the ones we invest the greatest time in developing and coaching to keep them engaged in their work, challenged, and consistently growing as employees. I bet you can already see how this applies to dating and relationships!

3. **Coaching and counseling:** Once we've looked at short-term performance and long-term potential, we have a pretty good sense of the value each employee adds to our widget organization. We can loosely group the employees into high performers, steady eddies, and under-performers. For our high performers, we think of them as the next generation of leadership. These rock stars just might run the widget factory some day! We coach them to further develop their skills, bring out the best in them, and retain them for the future.

Our steady eddies are important too. Not everyone needs to strive to be CEO. Then we'd have too many widget chiefs running around. We need dependable employees, subject matter experts, and people who keep the ship moving. So we coach this group to keep them interested in their work, happy and motivated. Instead of looking for promotional opportunities, we move employees in this group laterally, to keep their work fresh. So one year they're building widgets, the next they're selling them. They keep moving around, staying fresh and productive.

Finally, there are the underperformers, or the group that's not meeting expectations. Maybe our widget company isn't the best fit for their skills. Or they're in the wrong job at our firm. In either case, we work to improve their performance, either through more hands-on coaching or a job change. Hopefully they improve to the steady-eddie group or better. If not, we may consider moving them out to make room for recruiting fresh talent. Imagine having to tell an underperformer that they don't have what it takes to produce a fictional product like widgets. Wow, that must be a tough message to deliver!

## The SuperStar Network Speaks

Rather than just rely on our widget company to illustrate talent assessment, we checked in with our SuperStar Network of businesswomen and businessmen to get their perspective. Here's what they had to say about performance reviews, career potential analysis, and coaching.

1.  **Performance reviews:** Jorge, 41, stay-at-home dad: "Performance reviews play an important role in tracking progress and making adjustments for better performance—but most important, they provide an incentive for people to deliver on what they say they will deliver on. Written goals provide motivation for people to follow through."
2.  **Career potential analysis:** Chanice, 26, management trainee: "Past performance is the best predictor of future performance. So you can look at an employee's past three performance reviews to get an idea of long-term potential. But you also need to check if their last few jobs have maximized the unique strengths they bring to the table."
3.  **Coaching and counseling:** Julia, 33, marketing specialist: "Employee coaching can be used to address performance gaps, highlight specific development areas, and create a plan to close those gaps. The leader then provides continued coaching and feedback to the employee to ensure that performance stays on track."

### ···state of the business #8 ···············

By 2012, women are projected to earn nearly 57 percent of all advanced degrees in the U.S. alone. So success is booming in both business and education. Women are smart, successful, and savvy, and the facts continue to support it. When you proactively focus that same energy in a new direction, there's no reason dating results should fall short of the same success at work and academically.

# Stop Giving Me the Business

Okay, we've got all these terrific business tactics—now, let's look at Talent Assess-Men. You have this new e-mail from your boss:

> From: your.boss@work.com
> To: you@work.com
> Subject: Talent Assess-Men
> We got 2 rate your partners on their per4mance andd potential. Can u set it up?
> Tanks for making it happen.

We just learned how to rate employees on performance and potential. How can we now apply these tools to assess a guy you've been dating? It starts with the definition of Talent Assess-Men:

**JEFF'S DEF•I•NI•TIONS:** According to *Dating, Inc.*, Talent Assess-Men refers to the process of measuring a man's current dating performance versus future dating potential to determine the long-term value of the man to your relationship.

## Corporate Memo

TO: All Employees
FROM: Carol Cohen
RE: Your Love Life

Do you know that point in a relationship when it's time to have "the talk?" That's the point where we are in this book. Think about it. Why do you want to have "the talk" with the guy you're seeing? Usually it's because you're having a good time with him and now your thoughts have turned from recent performance to future potential. In other words, you're happy with the guy's performance so far. Now you're thinking about whether or not he has long-term potential. That's what companies consider for their employees, and you can do the same for that great guy you're dating. Is he a high performer, a steady eddie, or someone who needs to be managed out of your life? Let's find out!

## Let's Talk Performance (and We Don't Mean Between the Sheets)

Okay, performance in bed may be one of your important criteria, but let's take a broader perspective. How might you conduct a performance review on your man? Luckily, you're not starting from scratch here. This is your chance to go back and review all the great work you completed in previous chapters. I'm talking about your Wishin' Statement, Souls and Objectives, must-have, nice-to-have, and who-cares qualities. By now, you've gotten to know your man. How does he really stack up? To find out, let's play through the percentages. Let's look at how close your man comes to meeting 100 percent of what you desire in the Wishin' Statement, Souls and Objectives, and personal qualities.

### Wishin' Statement Review Time

I want you to go back and reread that Wishin' Statement you wrote, either in Chapter 1 or Appendix 1, wherever it's listed. Now I want you to answer three important yes or no questions. Don't think too hard, just circle yes or no, whichever seems right on gut instinct:

1. Does the guy you're currently dating seem like the guy described in your Wishin' Statement?
   **Yes**      No

2. Is the guy you're currently dating better than the guy you described in your Wishin' Statement?
   **Yes**      No

3. Could you see your guy eventually becoming, growing, or maturing into the guy you described in your Wishin' Statement?
   **Yes**      No

So how did you do? Do you have three "yes" answers, three "no" answers, or something in between? This is important because you probably haven't looked at that Wishin' Statement in awhile. Now reality is sinking in as you have to face whether or not your current boyfriend matches the qualities you visualized in the Wishin' Statement. If you have two or more "yes" responses, then you deserve some major reward and recognition. Pull out that old bottle of champagne stashed away in your cabinet, point it at your roommate, and spray her. (If you don't have a roommate, then ring your next-door neighbor's doorbell and go spray him.) This means that consciously or unconsciously, by setting a clear vision for yourself, you gravitated toward the right guy for what you're really seeking. If you have less than two "yes" responses, then it's gut check time. Should you be in a relationship with someone who's nothing like what you desire? Are you ignoring the writing on the wall?

## Corporate Memo

TO: All Employees
FROM: Carol Cohen
RE: Your Love Life

When I think about the different men I dated throughout my life (and let's face it, some of the really terrible ones should actually be referred to as boys), I stayed in the wrong relationship for so many reasons. Sometimes being with the wrong guy was better than being alone. Sometimes, despite repeated warnings from my friends and family, I continued to date the wrong person for me. Sometimes I thought he could be Mr. Right though I had never spent the time to really think about my own Wishin' Statement. In all of those cases, he turned out to be Mr. Going-Nowhere-Fast. Maybe it was my business training, all those years of writing visions, goals, and metrics, that finally taught me to be honest not just about my accomplishments on the job, but also on the singles scene. I finally woke up and realized that days spent with Mr. Wrong are at the expense of the search for Mr. Right! I know you can do this too. So if you just reread your Wishin' Statement, compared it to your current boyfriend, and realized they're miles apart, don't let it scare you. Instead let it empower you: you just had a major A-HA moment. I'm sure you have these moments all the time at the office. Now let's bring these A-HA moments right into your relationships and get Mr. Right moving up your corporate ladder or out the door!

## Wishin' Statement Sequel

Here's one more exercise to check how your guy compares to the one described in the Wishin' Statement. In the space provided below (or in the appendix) I want you to describe your current guy. Don't worry about what exactly should be included. Just put pen to paper right here, right now, and describe your man. Remember, honesty counts here, so don't intentionally try to make him sound like your Wishin' Statement. That's the *Dating, Inc.* equivalent of insider trading. Just write naturally what comes to you when you think about him.

_____

_____

_____

_____

Good work! Now we have your Wishin' Statement and this latest write-up to compare. The big million-dollar question becomes this: Does your current boyfriend described here sound anything like the guy described in your Wishin' Statement? Here's a scale to help you quantify this answer. I want you to put a mark somewhere on this scale from 0 to 100 percent. For this exercise, 0 percent indicates he is nothing like the one described in your Wishin' Statement. On the other end of the scale, 100 percent means your guy and the one described in the Wishin' Statement are almost identical.

Place your mark now, and then we'll interpret it together.

0%----------------------------50%--------------------------100%

So how did you do? I'm not that concerned with your precise answer. I just want to know if you're closer to the 0 or the 100? If he's close to the 100-percent mark, then you and I both know you've got a guy who sounds like the ideal type you've been seeking, the one who truly puts a smile on your face.

If he's more like 0 or 9 percent, then I'll bet you have friends and family already asking you the very question I'm going to ask you. Why are you still dating this guy?

## What's He Like? Who Cares!

Read that headline again. Pretend your best friend said to you, "What's he like?" in reference to the guy you're dating. Would you ever answer, "Who cares!" Of course not, it sounds preposterous. However, now is the time to think about your guy in greater detail. If he passed the Wishin' Statement test, how does he do in the must-have, nice-to-have, and who-cares list of qualities? Just as you did before, go back and look at that list of qualities you wrote up in the Souls and Objectives chapter. You just might find out that all the best qualities of your man fall under the "who-cares" list. Then again, you also might find out that he possesses all the must-have qualities you seek in a partner. There's only one way to find out. You've got to compare him to the chart you created in the Souls and Objectives chapter. This exercise won't require a doctorate in matchmaking—let's keep it simple. I want you to perform three easy steps:

1. Look at the list of must-have, nice-to-have, and who-cares qualities you created, and circle all the descriptions/preferences that sound like your guy. For example, the first trait on the list says "eye color." If you said you wanted blue eyes and he has blue eyes, circle that trait. If he has brown, hazel, or any other color but blue, don't circle the trait. Do this for the all of the traits on your list.

2. For all the traits you circled as matches, see how many are on your must-have, nice-to-have, or who-cares list. For example, if you wanted blue eyes, he has blue eyes, and this was listed as a nice-to-have quality, then that's one point for the nice-to-haves.

3. Add up your scores for must-have, nice-to-have, and who-cares. Be honest. How many of the traits and qualities you seek does he possess? Of the ones he possesses, how many fall under must-have, nice-to-have, or who-cares qualities?

**action item**

The Wishin' Statement provides some great insights into whether or not you're with the right guy. So does the must-have, nice-to-have, and who-cares chart. Use this information to your advantage and you'll quickly get some quality answers about the future you should have with your man. The chart lists twenty-one traits, not including any you may have added yourself. If your guy only has three of the twenty-one traits on your list, that says something. If your guy has nine of the twenty-one traits but all of them are on your who-cares list, that also says something. What does it say? It says you're with the wrong guy. On the flip side, if your guy does have lots of the traits and many fall in the nice-to-have and must-have categories, then you're on to something. If things don't work out, you now have all the tools you need to meet someone else, decide if you want to get serious and come right back to these tests to assess their long-term potential for that Mr. Right relationship opening! ❭

### He Potentially Has Potential

If your guy passes the Wishin' Statement test, meets your Souls and Objectives, and possesses a bunch of must-have traits, then in the business world it would all add up to a great performance review. In your love life, it's also a great indicator! As we learned earlier in this chapter, current performance is important, but so is long-term potential. That's why companies map performance against potential, looking for the highest performers: those who are great today and show signs of even more greatness in the years to come. So how do you apply this concept to the guy you're dating? It comes down to thinking ahead.

Allow me to give you ten questions you might want to ask yourself to see if he's got long-term potential:

1. Do you share similar values and morals?
2. Does he get along with your friends and family?
3. Do you have similar perspectives about finances and money management?
4. Would you want to live in similar parts of the world?
5. Are you of the same religion or could you exist as an interfaith couple?
6. Do you both want to have kids? Or could you accept existing children?
7. Do you share similar work ethics?
8. Do you have similar approaches to fitness and nutrition?

**9.** Are you compatible sexually?

**10.** Do you enjoy similar hobbies, activities, and interests?

Let's talk offline for a minute: promise me I didn't scare you with this list. I'm not asking you to hold a summit meeting with your guy to work through these topics. Instead, I'm just trying to point out that after you get past his current performance, you need to start considering longer-term questions to really understand the potential of the relationship. So while blue eyes and an athletic body may have been two must-have qualities for you, they won't hold up over the long term of a relationship. You'll eventually see that your opinions on topics like children and religion shift front and center. So all I'm asking you to do here is start asking yourself those deeper questions to really see if the connection is there for the future.

---

## Corporate Memo

TO: All Employees
FROM: Carol Cohen
RE: Your Love Life

---

If you've ever managed an employee, or even just thought about your own career potential within a company, then you've likely dealt with issues of performance and potential. That's the job of a manager, to assess the short-term and long-term value of an employee to the organization. However, there is a flip side to managing employees. While you're assessing them, they're also assessing you and the organization. You may think you have the control as the leader, but the employee can walk out the door at any time. The same holds true in relationships. While Jeff is talking about assessing your guy, we all know he's doing the same with you. He's thinking about the relationship, too, wondering if he sees Mrs. Right potential. Hopefully he's talking to you about this, but he also may be keeping it in his head or talking to his buddies about it. That got me thinking. Why do guys sometimes walk away from relationships? So I posed that very question to some of the insightful men and women from our SuperStar Network that we interviewed for the book. Here are three of the more interesting responses I received:

1. Amanda, 29, office manager from Oxford, England: "I've been dumped several times in situations where the guy just wasn't that into me. I probably came on too strong and the guy usually wasn't ready for something serious."
2. Evan, 44, investment banker from Sacramento, California: "A girl I dated in college had this male best friend who was clearly in love with her at the time. Though it was pretty clear that I was the love interest and he was the friend, our relationship was rocky and tumultuous. This other guy eventually drove us apart, and she married him a few years later, so I guess it was all for the best."
3. Ricky, 27, pharmacist from Nashville, Tennessee: "Any time a woman has left me it was clearly a failure of judgment on her part." Now that's some serious dating confidence! I'll bet he was in the wrong at least once or twice.

## From the Dating Trenches to the Relationship War Room

Let's say your guy passes the Wishin' Statement with flying colors. Let's also assume he's got many of the must-have qualities you desire. Finally, let's say that after asking yourself the longer-term questions, you start to see real potential. I'll bet there are still a few things about him that just plain bug you. Does he wear pleated khakis? Drive like a maniac? Revert to passive-aggressive tendencies when you argue? That's okay, we've all got some things that can get on each other's nerves. You just need to get comfortable addressing them so they don't end up turning into big deal-breakers. You want to avoid letting them get in the way of the long-term potential you see for the two of you. So how does a super-smart businesswoman like you bring up your man's little kinks without sending him running for the hills?

The answer lies in coaching and feedback. You do it all the time at work, so there's no reason you can't do it in relationships too. We've already talked about coaching and feedback in our Manage-Men chapter. However, as the relationship progresses, and you get to know each other better, the issues will change. The things that bother you in months one and two won't be the same as what gets to you at the three- or six-month mark. Even if they are the same, it was too early to really address them in months one or two. So how can a couple give each other feedback in the relationship without causing a breakup? Candice, an advertising executive from Scranton, Pennsylvania, shared a great concept from business, known as the war room, that can be applied to dating and relationships.

### Women's Intuition

According to Candice, "In advertising, the war room is used to hammer out an issue, to brainstorm, or solve a problem. For example, there's a new business pitch and the team assigned needs to get the juices flowing. They go into the war room and recruit anyone not on the project who has a free minute to go in to brainstorm. The rule is that there is no wrong answer. Every single idea that comes to mind, no matter how stupid it seems, should be voiced and will be up for consideration. In the dating world, every relationship needs a war room at some point. Maybe not necessarily the room itself, but what the room stands for—the ability to speak freely and have every idea be heard. This doesn't necessarily mean it only works for arguments . . . the war room concept could be applied for people getting to know each other. It's the idea that you can meet and just throw everything out there without feeling inhibited. It gives the pair the opportunity to speak openly without feeling embarrassed or hindering their ability to communicate out of fear of rejection."

## Let's Put It All Together Now

So what can we learn from performance reviews, career potential analysis, and coaching? Put them all together, and you have a great sense of whether or not to continue investing in a relationship. That's what companies do all the time with their employees to see if he's "the right man for the job," and you can do the same in dating to see if "he's the right man for a relationship." The importance of taking time in this step will become even more apparent in the next chapter, when we talk about joint ventures or Joint Adventures. That chapter will be about making life commitments with your guy. Before you even approach that step, you want to make sure he passes the Talent Assess-Men tests we outlined in this chapter. If so, you'll know you can move ahead with a clear head toward a stronger, long-lasting relationship commitment. If not, you'll be armed with the information you need to make the right decision about moving forward to find someone new. That's a perfect lead-in to the final concept I want to cover with you in this chapter: succession planning.

### Who Will Fill His Shoes?

Do you remember that pipeline, or steady stream, of talent we talked about in the Recruitment and Affection chapter? Now's the time to refresh your memory of what it takes to keep a consistent flow of great guys coming into your life. Now, if you've put your man through the Talent Assess-Men questions and tests and figured out that he's clearly the one, then this section is not for you. Move right on to the next chapter; you're ready for a Joint Adventure.

If, however, this chapter helped you realize you're with the wrong guy, then we both know it's time for you to end it. I know you'll find the courage to make this difficult move. Once you're single again, it will be important to get that pipeline up and running. I'm not talking about jumping full-steam ahead into a rebound relationship. By all means, take some time to decompress! But when you're ready to get back into the dating scene, succession planning will make all the difference for getting those initial dates to start rolling back in quickly.

According to the Society for Human Resources, succession planning is "the process of identifying long-range needs and cultivating a supply of internal talent to meet those future needs." So how does this apply to dating? Let's have Carol take the lead on this one since I've come to think of her as one of the most visionary, strategic businesswomen and exceptional people leaders that I've ever known. She networks with a lot of fantastic business people, jumps at the chance to work with new people all the time, and in some cases even makes a point not to lose touch with past SuperStars that worked for her.

## Corporate Memo

TO: All Employees
FROM: Carol Cohen
RE: Your Love Life

If it doesn't work out with one guy, it's easy to blame yourself and wonder what went wrong. These feelings are only natural. But think for a moment about your working career. I'll bet you've had to change jobs in the past when it wasn't working out with a particular company or leader. You didn't give up or blame yourself—you just moved on to a better fit. If you come to realize you're with the wrong guy, don't give up! Go back to your dating plan and keep trying. Now that you've learned all those proven business tactics to apply in your dating approach, it will be much easier. So just like in business when you need to find that "right man for the job," you can always reach out to your networks, open up the doors again to prospective candidates, and "find that right man for a relationship!" That's what succession planning is all about in dating and relationships. You keep that pipeline on the back burner while you're giving it a go with one guy. If it doesn't work out with him, then just like finding a new job, you pound the pavement again. Soon enough you'll be back to the Talent Assess-Men chapter with a new and even better man.

### Don't Play the Blame Game

The message that I hear from from the Corporate Memo is that this chapter is all about getting to the bottom of whether or not you have a good relationship fit. It's what you do all the time in business. You ask yourself whether a customer is a good fit for your product, even whether you are a good fit for your company.

By applying this same logic to the guy you're dating, you can make an informed decision about whether or not there's a real future together. If there is, then congratulate yourself for asking the tough questions to confirm what your heart is feeling. You've worked hard and earned the ultimate payoff! If the future just isn't there, then congratulate yourself again for finding that honesty and moving on from the wrong relationship. There might be some pain in that decision now, but the next great guy you meet will be oh so happy you're back on the market again.

## The Bottom Line

You're ready to move on to the next chapter if the following are true:

- You understand the business concepts of performance reviews, career potential analysis, and coaching.
- You know how these business concepts can be applied to your current relationship.
- You took the time to check the guy you're dating against your Wishin' Statement, Souls and Objectives, and must-have, nice-to-have, who-cares qualities.
- You've arrived at the right decision for you as to whether there's a real future for you and the guy you're dating.

# chapter nine

Biz Principle #9:
**Joint Venture**

Dating Principle #9:
**Joint Adventure**

## Agenda

- Why two companies enter into joint ventures
- How joint ventures in business relate to Joint Adventures in relationships
- Why every couple needs a relationship philosophy
- Words of wisdom from happily married couples

## Work/Life Balance

It's the end of another long and productive day. One of those days when you're really getting things done and the day just seems to fly. Your eye glances at the clock across your office. It's 6:27 P.M., time to shut down and head home. Commuting home, your mind wanders as you replay the events of the day. A smile spreads across your face as you reflect on a job truly well done. The scenery flies by as you cruise along the highway. Out of the corner of your eye, you barely catch a billboard just off the road. It's a word jumble, with one last message of motivation for you:

# DBLUI A FLEI RHEOETGT _____

This chapter more than any other is about teamwork. Leading up to this point, you've been working to meet great guys and figure out whether or not there's a future together. Now it's time to join forces with this great guy and enjoy the ride together! That's what this word jumble is all about, and it's the key message in this chapter.

---

## Corporate Memo

TO: All Employees
FROM: Carol Cohen
RE: Your Love Life

---

If you're reading this book straight through, then it's possible you haven't started your search yet for that wonderful partner. That's okay, there's nothing wrong with reading through the entire Dating Business Plan before getting started. After all, you're a super-savvy businesswoman, and you like to be informed before you jump into things. So if you're reading first and planning to take action later, I want you to really see this chapter as a source of aspiration. The Joint Adventure message that will be delivered here is all about the grand prize. Once you find that marvelous man and realize he's the one for you, then the time comes to create a fulfilling life together. The same way you'd work out a long-term career plan, this chapter will be about envisioning a life plan that the two of you will work out together. We've also included stories from real-life couples who found happiness and charted their course together, to inspire you. So as you read about them, let your mind run wild as you think about becoming one of those success stories. When you do ultimately put this Dating Business Plan in place and find your own great love, we want to hear about it. There's nothing more satisfying to us than hearing about your success story. It makes the journey so much more exciting and fulfilling. So get out there and date, build your life with the person you'll find, and tell us all about it at *contact@datingincbook.com.*

---

# Joint Ventures in Business

From: your.boss@work.com
To: you@work.com
Subject: Joint Venture
We r tinking of partnering with anutter company.
Whut will it take 2 be successful?
Tanks for making it happen.

So why do two companies choose to join forces? Typically, they both believe they can be more successful that way. They come to realize that their combined package can be a force to be reckoned with in the marketplace. If only it were easy for two companies to simply agree to work together. While the end result may be a powerhouse combination, it takes planning, communication, and compromise for the two companies to successfully partner—not unlike the merger of two like-minded folks in marriage. Let's break it down from a business perspective, and then we'll turn our attention to dating.

> **JEFF'S DEF•I•NI•TIONS:** According to Wikipedia, a joint venture is a strategic alliance between two or more parties to undertake economic activity together.

## To Succeed or Not Succeed, That Is the Question

Success for any joint venture relies on three key elements, or as I like to call them, the three "C's":

1. **Communicate:** First, each business needs to communicate their individual goals and what they hope to achieve by joining forces.
2. **Compromise:** Second, the two businesses need to compromise on their individual goals until they arrive at and agree upon joint goals.

3. **Conquer:** Finally, once the two businesses are on the same page in their business goals, they can enter and hopefully conquer the marketplace together.

Let's talk offline for a minute: communicate, compromise, conquer. I'm sure there would be more "C's" and maybe a few additional letters if we really broke down what it takes to implement a successful joint venture in business. When the two companies involved are multinational corporations, there are all kinds of logistics involved. But for the purposes of this book, let's keep it simple. Business (and relationships) can be complicated enough!

### Adventures in Ventures

As usual, leave it to our SuperStar Network to put the connections between joint ventures in business and Joint Adventures in dating and relationships in perspective. Gary, a forty-four-year-old sociology professor from Santa Fe, New Mexico, mentioned the importance of synergy in successful ventures, both at work and in relationships.

"While the term 'synergy' is often overused in the business world today, at its core it is about two companies coming together to create something that is more than the sum of what they were by themselves. In a good relationship, while a little bit of each individual (the 'I') may be lost, the team that is created (the 'we') more than makes up for it."

## Are You Adventuresome?

So what happens when we apply the business concept of joint ventures to the relationship concept of Joint Adventures? Let's start as always with the new e-mail from your boss.

From: your.boss@work.com
To: you@work.com
Subject: Joint Adventure
If ur tinking of partnering with anutter person, whut will it take 2 be successful?
Tanks for making it happen.

Remember, at this point we're not necessarily talking engagement and marriage. We are, however, way beyond a casual relationship. We're talking about a committed, monogamous relationship that you both hope will lead to a lifetime together. Hopefully the Talent Assess-Men chapter helped you determine if in fact you see a bright future together. This chapter will help you focus on building a life together. Let's begin with the definition of a Joint Adventure.

**JEFF'S DEF•I•NI•TIONS:** According to *Dating, Inc.* a Joint Adventure is a strategic alliance between two people to undertake a life together.

### Requirements for a Successful Joint Adventure

Couples spend months planning their wedding. They worry over every last detail of the cake, the band, the flowers, the food. It's only natural to feel that trepidation as the big day approaches. All of your friends and family will be present; you don't want to embarrass yourself in front of everyone you know.

What if these same couples put the same time and energy into planning the rest of their lives together? Again, we're not assuming you're engaged or getting married to your potential Mr. Right at this point. Of course, if you are, then congratulations to you and your great guy. However, even if you're not ready to talk about the ultimate commitment, this stage in your relationship does require talking about more than just where to have dinner tonight. You need to start getting into topics such as finances, religion, values, kids, family, and so on.

To get the dialogue going, Carol and I enlisted the help of husband and wife team, Judith Sherven, Ph.D. and James Sniechowski, Ph.D. As bestselling authors and internationally acclaimed teleseminar teachers, Judith and Jim have redefined success in relationships. We consider them *Dating, Inc.* advisors, and interviewed Judith and Jim to get their perspectives on planning a life together. The following is an excerpt from the interview.

**Question #1:** Couples spend months planning every last detail of their wedding, but often little time planning the rest of their lives together. If a couple wants to apply the same strategic planning they do for their "big day" to every other day of their life together, what topics do you believe they should discuss?

**Judith and Jim:** This is what we call "Popping the Questions," and we suggest that every couple make a point of discussing the following ten key marriage issues before even considering a formal union:

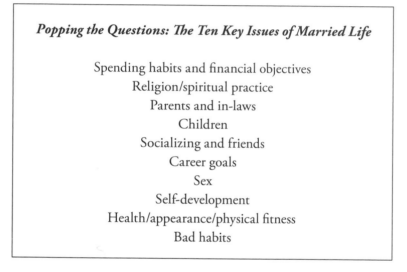

*Popping the Questions: The Ten Key Issues of Married Life*

Spending habits and financial objectives
Religion/spiritual practice
Parents and in-laws
Children
Socializing and friends
Career goals
Sex
Self-development
Health/appearance/physical fitness
Bad habits

During these conversations, there will be some moments where you feel relaxed, elated even, to think of the ways in which you're alike. You're also bound to be surprised, maybe even shocked, when you realize how different the two of you are, no matter how much you may have in common. Don't worry and don't fret when you hit these rougher patches. It's only in your differences that the depth of real intimacy is possible.

By holding these conversations and negotiating any differences that emerge, whether or not you're planning to marry, you develop the skills of self-expression, deep listening, and mutually beneficial conflict resolution, confirming your readiness for a deeper commitment.

To accomplish this, each person must express his or her side of the "problem" while the other listens and learns. Once they both have a fundamental grasp of both sides, they experience what we call "The Magic of Differences." Then they can begin to integrate what they've learned, recognize the assets that they each bring to the issue (and the distortions or misunderstandings they've held), and join together to create a new way of relating.

**Question #2:** Where do couples sometimes go wrong in planning their lives together? How can they avoid these common pitfalls?

**Judith and Jim:** The number one mistake both women and men make is to assume that their partner knows what they feel, want, or need. No matter how long a couple has been together, no matter how sensitive or "psychic" someone may be, the leading problem that brings couples in for counseling is that they have failed to share, understand, and integrate what is important to each of them as individuals and to both of them as a couple.

The primary idea that you need to keep in mind is that your partner is not you. Second, each of you must hold the well-being of your relationship as your highest priority. In other words, rather than try to win or dominate, you must opt for what will strengthen and deepen your connection. With these two commitments in mind and heart, when difficult times arise, and they will, neither of you will revert to the position, "I'm looking out for me." You'll be looking out for your relationship and, by doing so, you will be looking out for each other.

**Question #3:** How can family and close friends help and/or hurt a couple's efforts to establish a life together? What tips can you give couples to stay close to friends and family during and after this transition to a committed relationship?

**Judith and Jim:** Family and friends need to remember that their relationship to the couple is now secondary to the couple's commitment to their own relationship. That means that, as family or friend, you will never assume that you have special rights just because you are a parent, sibling, or friend, or that your relationship with one or both of them predates the new couple.

**Question #4:** How can couples tap into each other's natural strengths to work together as a team in life?

**Judith and Jim:** One of the blessings of being in a committed relationship is that there's more than one person to take care of things. So, rather than try to control everything, determine who is naturally inclined toward doing things like paying the bills. Who likes to keep an eye on automobile upkeep? Which of you tends to make social plans, clean the garage, do the laundry, and keep lists of what needs to get done? Who leads in the playful department? Who's the visionary? And so on. And be sure not to assume old gender stereotypes. She may be the mechanic and he may be the social plan maker.

**Question #5:** How do you avoid letting personality differences constantly cause relationship stress?

**Judith and Jim:** The key is to always remember that your lover's habits, feelings, and behaviors are as important to him or her as yours are to you. Now, that doesn't mean you can't ask for change. But, bottom line, one of the most powerful psychological challenges provided by a committed relationship is that each of us has to come to grips with our own narcissism—that belief that our way is the best way, and that our partner needs to get on program and think and feel just like we do. The key is to honor and value our own and each other's different ways. Only then can we enjoy the love we so desire—to be loved for who we really are and love our partner in just the same way.

···**state of the business #9** ···············
The growth rate for women in the U.S. workforce is almost one-third higher than that for men. Just because women are taking a bigger role in the workplace, it doesn't have to be at the expense of a love life. That's what this dating plan is all about!

# The Relationship Philosophy

I like to ask as many couples as I can, "What's your relationship philosophy?" No, I don't walk up to total strangers and blurt out this question. Rather, when I'm at informal dinners with friends or leading a seminar for couples, I pose this question. When couples understand the question and share their approach in tackling life together, it brings a smile to my face. I know that this is a couple with a great shot of lasting over time. On the other hand, sometimes I'm met with blank stares and it's obvious the couples have never broached the subject together.

A relationship philosophy is all about the strategy behind a Joint Adventure. If two people choose to tackle life's ups and downs together, what is their joint philosophy on life's biggest categories (such as money, children, religion, family)?

## The ABCs of a Relationship Philosophy

As a way to expound on the joys and importance of a relationship philosophy, I've enlisted the help of Andrea and Ralph Stanton, a newlywed couple from San Francisco, California. A couple of years ago, Andrea and Ralph approached me to help them write a relationship philosophy. They had swapped wedding vows three months prior and were ready to tackle life together. Though they were smart enough to realize that it had to be done, discussing finances, love, kids, family, hobbies, career, and so on felt completely overwhelming to them. I see this with many couples: They know they need to have the important life discussions, they *want* to have the important life discussions, but the topics are so broad, it's impossible to figure out where to start. All you really need to do, though, is to take an overwhelming topic like life planning, remove the intimidation, and break it down into easy-to-follow steps. I'm going to show you how it's done. For Andrea and Ralph, I gave them three straightforward assignments:

1.  First, take time individually to write where you each want to be one year from now, in five years, ten years, twenty-five years, and fifty years for each of the key life topics (career,

family, finances, love, etc.). Do not share your responses in this step.

2. Now share your responses and merge your individual responses into one combined draft. As you might imagine, compromise is key here. If one person envisioned eight kids and the other none, you have some talking to do.

3. Once some agreement has been reached on the life plan, the third step is all about converting the vision into an action plan with steps to make the dream a reality.

---

## Corporate Memo

TO: All Employees
FROM: Carol Cohen
RE: Your Love Life

---

Three steps, yes, but it does take some time to work through these steps, particularly step two. As you can imagine, this step takes an investment of time. It's not as easy as writing it all up alone. But, then again, the purpose of a Joint Adventure is so you don't have to go at it alone.

Jeff and I followed his own advice when we got married, and let me tell you, when we completed our separate relationship philosophies and compared our notes, it was both rewarding and scary. The exercise was rewarding in that many of our values, hopes, and dreams overlapped. We both wanted to run a business together, we both wanted a big family, we both wanted health and nutrition to be important parts of our lives. On the flip side, Jeff wanted to live in the city, whereas I envisioned a more rural home. Jeff wanted two kids; I came from a big family where my father has eleven brothers and sisters. Needless to say, it took many deep conversations and a few not-so-nice discussions to get on the same page. But I really believe the time we invested early in our relationship has paid huge dividends today. We're aligned on the most important goals in our lives and that means we can work as a team, a true unit, not against each other.

---

### Steps 1, 2, and 3 Come to Life for Andrea and Ralph

If only we had time to share everything Andrea and Ralph came up with in all the key categories. It would be a fascinating journey into what it takes to plan a future together. For now, let's just look at how they managed the finance aspect of their relationship philosophy. This is a great example, because we all know money is the number-one thing that couples fight about and a reason that couples often cite when filing for divorce.

### Step 1—Individual Visions of Finance

Now remember, Andrea and Ralph were each asked to write their visions for their finances one year out, five years out, in ten years, twenty-five years, and fifty years. Let's just look at their individual write-ups for one year out to keep this example simple:

#### In One Year, Ralph and I Will:

- Have developed a realistic budget that allows us to make payments on accrued debt, as well as still enjoy some little luxuries (such as a weekend getaway)
- Be actively saving money for annual vacations
- Have prioritized where we want to spend our money
- Each know how much money we have, and how much debt we have
- No longer spend frivolously!
- Have joint checking and savings accounts
- Have a clear financial plan and be comfortable discussing money

#### In One Year, Andrea and I Will:

- Be on a budget and keeping close tabs on our monthly spending
- Have figured out how much of our monthly income goes toward necessities and how much goes toward entertainment
- Have decided that the following are necessities: mortgage, car, gas, electric, home insurance, car insurance, personal property insurance, groceries, certain clothing expenses, home maintenance

- Have discussions on everything else to see how important they are to our way of life, then put together a spreadsheet that compiles all the information and the cost associated with it, to see how much we need to save and how much extra we will have. This will help us budget our money when we start our family. We are in debt and need to be conscious of how we spend our money.

Let's talk offline for a minute: remember, Andrea and Ralph did not work together on these finance visions. As you read them, I'll bet you can see areas where they're on the same page versus areas that will require some serious discussion. For example, they both want a budget and want to get out of debt. Those are important and aligned goals. Imagine if one wanted a budget and no debt while the other preferred to maintain a free-spending lifestyle with no plans to pay off school loans.

On the flip side, Andrea highlights the need for joint accounts. This is not on Ralph's radar screen. Ralph mentions the idea of starting a family as it relates to a realistic budget. Andrea doesn't even seem to be thinking kids yet. The good news is that Andrea and Ralph are getting these discrepancies on the table now, before they head too far down independent paths in the same life.

### Step 2—Let's Get on the Same Page

After Andrea and Ralph finished their independent assignments, it was time to share their answers. At this point, I urged Andrea and Ralph to get a nice bottle of wine and settle in for round two, reaching a unified vision, of their relationship philosophy on finance. I told them to avoid squaring off for a heavyweight title fight or a corporate negotiation. They had to remember at all times that they're on the same team, trying to build a life together.

Following is what they came up with as their unified financial vision for one year.

**Andrea and Ralph's Combined Financial Vision for One Year from Now:**

- We have met with a financial planner and are becoming more financially smart.
- We have begun investing more.
- We have developed a realistic budget that allows us to make payments on accrued debt, as well as still enjoy some little luxuries (such as a weekend getaway).
- We keep close tabs on our monthly spending, understanding what we need for food, clothing, entertainment, etc.
- We are actively saving money for annual vacations, and prioritized where we want to spend our money.
- We no longer spend frivolously!
- We have joint checking and savings accounts, along with one individual checking.
- We have a clear financial plan and are comfortable discussing money.
- We each know how much money we have, and how much debt we have.
- We are aware of our debt.

Well, well, well, what do we have here? You'll see that some of Andrea and Ralph's independent ideas found their way into the combined draft. You'll also see instances where their combined thinking created a new idea. For example, both of them wanted to get smarter with their finances. However, only when they shared their drafts together did they arrive at the idea of meeting with a financial planner. Now that proves why two heads are better than one!

### Step 3—A Vision Without Action Is Like a Ship Without a Destination

Now that Andrea and Ralph know what they want out of their finances, the key is to turn this vision into actionable steps. These actions are the means to make their game plan a reality. So let's see how Andrea and Ralph broke down one of their goals, to get smarter about money and start investing.

| Finances | | | |
|---|---|---|---|
| **Invest- ments** | **Vision for One Year from Now** • We have met with a financial planner and are becoming more financially smart. • We have a clear financial plan and are comfortable discussing money. • We have begun investing more. | | |
| | **Actions:** | **Due Date** | **Accountability** |
| | • Research 3-5 potential financial planners | 5 Nov | Ralph |
| | • Schedule introductory meetings with potential financial planners | 11 Nov | Andrea |
| | • Jointly attend all introductory meetings to interview financial planners | 20 Nov | Both |
| | • Choose best financial planner (or interview more if necessary) | 1 Dec | Both |
| | • Jointly determine how much to initially invest with chosen financial planner | 15 Dec | Both |
| | • Meet with financial planner to deposit initial investment and discuss long-term financial planning (i.e., insurance, children, graduate school) | 31 Dec | Both |

How about a round of applause for Andrea and Ralph? Remember, they came to me as newlyweds, excited about their future together, but overwhelmed by the prospect of making decisions in major life categories. Before they married, they had been together over five years and never truly broke down any of these major topics together. Now, they're planning in a three-week period to research potential financial planners, interview the best of the bunch, choose one to start working with, and start investing. Now that is a couple that is on the Bold Road of life, ready to begin their journey together!

{ I definitely told Andrea and Ralph to rejoice in making a relationship philosophy together. At the same time, I reminded them of the importance of revisit-
ing this plan every year or so. Life moves fast, and relationship philosophies are
not intended to be static documents. So don't file them away with your old tax
returns. Keep your relationship philosophy front and center in your life and adjust
it as life priorities change for you and Mr. Right. }

## Now You Be Andrea

You've had a chance to read through an example from Andrea and
Ralph on their relationship philosophy for finances in one year. Now
it's your turn. Before you jump in, I want to recognize the fact that you
may be reading this book straight through cover to cover. If that's the
case, then you may not have even begun your search for Mr. Right.
That's okay. There's nothing wrong with digesting the material before
you jump into action. If you're in reading mode right now and plan to
act later, then keep this section handy for when you do find the right
guy. I know you will, by the way. Or you could get a jump on things
by filling out your individual sections now. On the flip side, if you've
been following the steps in this book as you read, then hopefully you're
even reading this section with your Mr. Right and are ready to tackle a
relationship philosophy together. So let's get to work.

### Step 1—Your Independent Goals

You hopefully remember the key issues Judith and Jim recommended tackling in their interview earlier in this chapter. Carol and
I also have our own list, consisting of nine key life categories. (Everything is about the number nine with us, probably because we met on
the ninth of January and got married on the ninth of November.) Our
nine categories are love, career, health, finances, family, home, friendships, personal development, and values. You can go with our list,
Judith and Jim's, or make one of your own. The key is that you and
your partner individually write where you want to be in life in each
category for five life stages, one year out, five years, ten years, twenty-
five years, and fifty years. These don't have to be long write-ups, just a
paragraph for each life stage and life category. Remember, no cheating

off each other's papers—this is an independent assignment for now. To help you out, here's a quick template breaking down how you would fill one of the categories, having children:

In one year, here's my vision for our approach to having and raising children:

_____

In five years, here's my vision for our approach to having and raising children:

_____

In ten years, here's my vision for our approach to having and raising children:

_____

In twenty-five years, here's my vision for our approach to having and raising children:

_____

In fifty years, here's my vision for our approach to having and raising children:

_____

As a reminder, you would fill this template out yourself, and your main squeeze would do the same on a separate sheet of paper. Then you would repeat this process for the other life categories. Got it? Now let's see what you come up with!

## Corporate Memo

TO: All Employees
FROM: Carol Cohen
RE: Your Love Life

Don't forget your business skills here. If you think you've never done this before, think again! By now, you have hopefully learned from *Dating, Inc.*

that your dating arsenal is full of knowledge you learned along the way in business, whether it was your first job as a babysitter or your current one as a SuperStar. Pretend for a moment the topic wasn't having and raising children, rather revenue. I'll bet you could write a vision for what your company wanted to achieve in revenue over the next one, five, ten, twenty-five, and fifty years. Use that same business mindset here. Think from a success-oriented, achievement perspective. Do you want to have kids together? If so, how many? Don't worry—this is not set in stone, it's just a vision representing how you feel at this moment in time. Will you have a strict or lenient household? Will your kids go to public or private school? Think big here. That's what a vision is all about. In the next two steps you'll have a chance to compromise with Mr. Right and create the action plan. So for now, don't hold back. What do you really want out of your life categories?

---

### Step Two—He Said, She Said

Now that you've written your independent visions, it's time to play nice together and come up with a unified vision for each life category at each life stage. The goal here is to have one write-up that you both agree on and will champion together. Remember, this is a Joint Adventure, so it can't be all about what you want as an individual. This step requires reading each other's visions with an open mind, having comfortable discussions on the areas where you disagree, and eventually arriving at a unified game plan. Please, no fighting during this step—you're trying to build a life together. Leverage the same skills you would to get along with colleagues in the business setting.

Ultimately, you should have the same goals to rise above the competition and be one of the long-lasting companies in the marketplace. The same business tactic applies in your relationship. Find a way to work together as a team, not against each other as competitors. You too want to become one of the long-lasting relationships out there. To help you out, go back and read Andrea and Ralph's finance write-ups and how they came together to write one, unified plan. Here's a template you can fill in together when you're ready, again using the "children" example. After you fill this in, you would then duplicate this process for the other life categories under discussion.

Our joint vision of where we'll be in one year in regard to having and raising children:

_____

Our joint vision of where we'll be in five years in regard to having and raising children:

_____

Our joint vision of where we'll be in ten years in regard to having and raising children:

_____

Our joint vision of where we'll be in twenty-five years in regard to having and raising children:

_____

Our joint vision of where we'll be in fifty years in regard to having and raising children:

_____

### Step 3—Take Those Baby Steps Together

At this point, the two of you are on the same page, and that's a great place to be. Now all you have to do is convert the joint vision into action steps and make it happen. So build on what you saw Andrea and Ralph do, and you'll be on your way. Let's say you have a joint vision for the next year to get pregnant and have your first baby. This goal could be broken down into the following actions:

- Choose a gynecologist or fertility doctor to begin the process.
- Get tested to make sure you don't have any health issues.
- Read two books about getting pregnant and what to expect.
- Create an intimate atmosphere at home that fosters baby making.
- Buy an ovulation kit to help predict the best times to have sex.

You get the idea, and again, we're not asking you to treat baby making as a business transaction. All we're saying is to take a broad vision like getting pregnant and break it down to the point that each of the individual steps does not feel overwhelming. You can create a template similar to Andrea and Ralph's or design one yourself. The key is to list the visions action steps, due date, and accountability. That way you'll know what you're trying to get done, the steps to get there, when it's due, and who's doing what. Here's a simple template you can follow:

| Relationship Philosophy Action Plan | | | |
|---|---|---|---|
| **Life Category:** | **Visions:**<br>• Vision #1 is:_____<br><br>_____<br><br>• Vision #2 is:_____<br><br>_____<br><br>• Vision #3 is:_____<br><br>_____ | | |
| | **Actions:**<br>Action #1 is: _____<br><br>_____<br>Action #2 is: _____<br><br>_____<br>Action #3 is: _____<br><br>_____<br>Action #4 is: _____<br><br>_____ | **Due Date** | **Accountability** |

## Corporate Memo

TO: All Employees
FROM: Carol Cohen
RE: Your Love Life

We all get overwhelmed sometimes when we have to convert our visions into actions and reality. It's only natural to feel that twinge of nervousness in your stomach as you think about pulling off a vision. But how do you do this at work? You break down that vision into small chunks and keep breaking it down until the actions you have to take in and of themselves do not overwhelm you. That's all you have to do here. If getting in shape, changing careers, investing smarter, or reconnecting with family members scares you, take control of that fear and break it down until the action items are so simple, so straightforward, that you're not afraid to jump in and get started. Pretty soon you'll be on your way to making it happen!

## Couple's Intuition

Throughout this book, we've shared countless examples of Women's Intuition. These sections are all meant to bring to life the very theories we share in *Dating, Inc.* Since this chapter is about making it work as a couple, we reached out to our SuperStar Network and looked for couples who really know how to make their Joint Adventure work. So here's their best advice on starting a life together.

### John and Lonetta, Alpharetta, Georgia

We met with my rabbi to discuss various marital topics before our wedding. We met with her about four or five times. I found three of the topics she had us discuss very helpful:

- **Money:** How important is it? Will one of us stay home with the kids, or do we see ourselves being a dual income family, etc.?
- **Family:** Do we want to have kids, important things about raising children, etc.? One question she asked us while we were discussing family has always stuck with me. She asked us individually to come up with a quality about our parent's relationship we want to copy, and one that we do not want to take into our marriage.
- **Negotiations:** Methods on working out conflict in marriage and how to fight constructively.

### Maria and Enrique, Madrid, Spain

The key is expectations! Understanding expectations of the sexual relationship, financial future, family desires, daily life, and how compromises that may arise will be handled. I think that many relationships fail because one or the other partner's expectations are not met, but maybe those expectations were never discussed ahead of time. Lay it all out, and be willing and able to make adjustments along the way. We all have an image of what the future will be like, and believe me, it is never exactly what you imagine it will be. Be willing to meet your partner in the moment (I'm thinking future moments—like through the years into a marriage). Being realistic about how expectations must change as your life unfolds is critical. Holding on to unrealistic expectations will doom you to go from relationship to relationship and be disappointed by every one of them. Real-life relationships are hard work; real life is hard work.

### Nina and Charles, Vancouver, Canada

The quality most critical to a business relationship surviving in the long run is trust. In my profession, we hear over and over that clients know there are many good law firms who can handle their work. We try to separate ourselves from our competition by creating relationships in which there is trust in us as individuals. Similarly, in romantic relationships, a person may be incredibly intelligent, attractive, and all these other things. But if that person cannot be trusted, I don't see how the relationship is going to work.

### Van and Ricky, New York, New York

Hopefully, most important topics have been covered way before the wedding day comes. However, I think it's important to talk about the couple's personal goals. It's important to understand each person's career goals and priorities over the next five years and beyond. You may find that your priorities are similar, or that they are very different. If they are similar, that's great. Then it's just a matter of figuring out how to attain the goals and the timing of them. If they are different, you have to work together to prioritize. One person's goals may have to be pushed off for the other person's. Once you start your life together, everything impacts your quality of life. Where you live, when you start a family, how many children you want, how you spend your first five years together all shape what kind of future you'll share. As hard as it is, the sooner you start talking about your finances, the better. Are you going to share checking accounts? Will everything be joint, or will you each have separate accounts as well? Do you have debt? How much?

You need to start attacking all of your financial issues together so you can start building a solid financial ground to build your life on.

## The Bottom Line

So what's the bottom line? Well, it's easy to think the work in dating is all about finding the right guy. Then it's clear sailing. But as you can see from our SuperStar Network, there's much to do once you find that special someone. So if you've followed the tips in this book and found the right guy for you, don't let the work stop. Build a relationship philosophy together, and you'll build a life together!

You're ready to move on to the closing remarks in *Dating, Inc.* if the following are true:

- You understand what it takes for a company to succeed when it merges together with another company.
- You see the connection between ventures in business and adventures in relationships.
- You're excited to dive into a relationship philosophy with your partner and make your joint dreams into a reality.

# conclusion
# closing remarks

Let me be the first to congratulate you for making it to the closing remarks. You clearly turned out to be the SuperStar, savvy woman I knew you could be. Best of all, you now know exactly how to apply the business principles you already use at work to land a great guy. I want to conclude by piecing together the word jumbles you completed throughout this book. Together they form a motivational roadmap that I know will guide you successfully on your journey. Here's the recap. If you remember nothing else from this book, I hope you keep these motivational messages front and center in your search for the wonderful man you deserve.

Word Jumble #1:  Enjoy the Ride
Word Jumble #2:  Shoot for the Stars
Word Jumble #3:  Get off the Sidelines
Word Jumble #4:  Be Honest with Yourself
Word Jumble #5:  Make Your Own Action
Word Jumble #6:  Go Find Your Man
Word Jumble #7:  See the Real Him
Word Jumble #8:  Make Him Lust After You
Word Jumble #9:  Love Him or Leave Him
Word Jumble #10:  Build a Life Together

## Corporate Memo

TO: All Employees
FROM: Carol Cohen
RE: Your Love Life

Throughout this book, my goal has been to be your unconditional cheer-leader. I know how hard we've battled as women to break through the glass ceiling. As we continue to land CEO jobs, start new businesses, and make our mark in the business world, it's important to never forget the balance of success at work versus a fulfilled family life. To me, that's what this book is all about. We're not trying to catapult our business success at the expense of a romantic success. Instead, it's all about having both our business life and dating life firing on all cylinders. I hope you walk away from this book seeing how the very tools you use to be successful at work will make all the difference as you conquer the dating world. Now go out there and find the right man for you. He's ready and waiting and now you've got everything you need to get out there and find him!

## Carol and Jeff Unite

Together we want to close by thanking you for inviting us into your life. Whether you read this book late at night, on the train, or at your local bookstore, you devoted your precious time to hear our message. For that, we are forever grateful. We truly hope you find the great guy you deserve.

Your commitment to read this book is a great first step. You are officially on the Bold Road of life. Now take that second step and find your man! We can't wait to hear your success stories at *contact@ datingincbook.com*.

# bibliography

Ford Motor Company information retrieved on January 15, 2006 from *www.ford.com.au/global/pdf/content/6.pdf*

General Electric company information retrieved on January 15, 2006 from *www.ge.com/en/company*

Google mission statement retrieved on January 15, 2006 from *www .google.com/intl/en/corporate/index.html*

Investorwords.com. Research and Development definition retrieved on January 15, 2006 from InvestorWords.com at *www.investorwords .com/4200/research_and_development.html*

Society for Human Resource Management. Definitions of vision statement, goals, objectives, employer of choice, recruitment, performance management, and succession planning retrieved on January 15, 2006 from the Society for Human Resource Management at *http://shrm .org/hrresources/hrglossary_published*

Wikipedia. Customer Service definition retrieved on January 15, 2006 from Wikipedia.com at *http://en.wikipedia.org/wiki/Customer_service*

Wikipedia. Joint Venture definition retrieved on January 15, 2006 from Wikipedia.com at *http://en.wikipedia.org/wiki/Joint_venture*

Wikipedia. Marketing Plan definition retrieved on January 15, 2006 from Wikipedia.com at *http://en.wikipedia.org/wiki/Marketing_plan*

Catalyst. Statistics retrieved from Catalyst Information Center on January 15, 2006. Original data retrieved from:

State of the Business #1: Current Population Statistics, Families and Living Arrangements, "Table A1. Marital Status of People of 15 Years and Over, by Age, Sex, Personal Earnings, Race."

State of the Business #2: Jason Fields, America's Families and Living Arrangements: 2003 Current Population Reports. *www.census.gov/prod/2004pubs/p20-553.pdf*

State of the Business #3: Bureau of Labor Statistics, Women in the Labor Force: A Databook, "Table 4. Employment status by marital status and sex, 2002 annual averages."

State of the Business #4: Bureau of Labor Statistics, "Highlights of Women's Earnings in 2003," September 2004. *www.bls.gov/cps/cpswom2003.pdf*

State of the Business #5: Center for Women's Business Research, "Completing the Picture: Equally-Owned Firms in 2002" (April 2003).

State of the Business #6: Catalyst, Women in U.S. Corporate Leadership 2003.

State of the Business #7: 2002 Catalyst Census of Women Corporate Officers and Top Earners in Fortune 500.

State of the Business #8: NCES, 2002 ("advanced degrees" refers to master's, first-professional, and doctoral degrees).

State of the Business #9: Howard J. Fullerton Jr. and Mitra Toosi, "Labor Force Projections to 2010: Steady Growth and Changing Composition." *Monthly Labor Review* (November 2001):32.

# your personal dating business plan

Here's your chance to put it all together. You've seen business plans before, but this one is all about dating. So fill in your Dating Business Plan based on the principles taught in *Dating, Inc.* and you'll be on your way to finding and keeping a great guy.

## Dating Principle #1—Wishin' Statement

A Wishin' Statement refers to what a single woman wants to find on the dating scene or hopes to accomplish in a future relationship.

_____

_____

_____

_____

_____

## Dating Principle #2—Souls and Objectives

Must-have, nice-to-have, and who-cares qualities help narrow your laundry list of traits and qualities to the ones that matter most in finding a great guy. For each characteristic write your preference/description, put a check mark in the box under the "Must Have," "Nice to Have," or "Who Cares" columns to indicate your preference. Then, at the bottom of the chart, add up the total checks for each column to get your score.

**Must-Have/Nice-to-Have/Who-Cares Chart**

| Characteristic | Your Preference/Description | Must Have | Nice to Have | Who Cares |
|---|---|---|---|---|
| **Physical Traits** Eye Color Hair Color Height Weight Body Type Age Range Other | | | | |
| **Descriptive Traits** Race Religion Smoking Drinking Pets Education Career Other | | | | |
| **Intangible Traits** Ambition Patience Sense of Humor Communication Listening Skills Sexual Chemistry Family Closeness Desire for Kids Other | | | | |
| **Total Checks** | | | | |

## Dating Principle #2—Souls and Objectives (continued)

Here's where you bring your Wishin' Statement and must-have, nice-to-have, who-cares write-ups to life. Write your top overall dating goal, followed by five sub-goals that you know would move you closer to accomplishing your main dating goal.

## Top Dating Goal

My top dating goal is to: _____

_____

_____

## Dating Sub-goals

Sub-goal #1 _____

_____

Sub-goal #2 _____

_____

Sub-goal #3 _____

_____

Sub-goal #4 _____

_____

Sub-goal #5 _____

_____

## Dating Principle #2—Souls and Objectives (continued)

Sub-goals rarely get done without deadlines and milestones. So for each of your sub-goals, give yourself a deadline and write three milestones that will keep you on track to accomplish your sub-goal by the due date.

I will achieve sub-goal #1 by: _____

Here are three milestones that will keep me on track for sub-goal #1:

**1.** _____

_____

**2.** _____

_____

**3.** _____

_____

I will achieve sub-goal #2 by: _____

Here are three milestones that will keep me on track for sub-goal #2:

1. _____

_____

2. _____

_____

3. _____

_____

I will achieve sub-goal #3 by: _____

Here are three milestones that will keep me on track for sub-goal #3:

1. _____

_____

2. _____

_____

3. _____

_____

I will achieve sub-goal #4 by: _____

Here are three milestones that will keep me on track for sub-goal #4:

1. _____

_____

2. _____

_____

3. _____

_____

I will achieve sub-goal #5 by: _____

Here are three milestones that will keep me on track for sub-goal #5:

**1.** _____

_____

**2.** _____

_____

**3.** _____

_____


### Dating Principle #2—Souls and Objectives (continued)

Metrics or success measures help us know if our goals have accomplished what we set out for them to do in the first place. Here's your chance to write the quantitative and qualitative metrics that will tell you whether each sub-goal is on track.

Three quantitative or qualitative metrics that will help me measure my success for sub-goal #1 are:

**1.** _____

_____

**2.** _____

_____

**3.** _____

_____

Three quantitative or qualitative metrics that will help me measure my success for sub-goal #2 are:

1. _____

_____

2. _____

_____

3. _____

_____


Three quantitative or qualitative metrics that will help me measure my success for sub-goal #3 are:

1. _____

_____

2. _____

_____

3. _____

_____


Three quantitative or qualitative metrics that will help me measure my success for sub-goal #4 are:

1. _____

_____

2. _____

_____

3. _____

_____

Three quantitative or qualitative metrics that will help me measure my success for sub-goal #5 are:

1. _____

_____

2. _____

_____

3. _____

_____

## Dating Principle #3— Research and Envelopment

Research starts with the current state of affairs. So let's hear it. Why do you personally believe you're successful at work but haven't found that great guy yet?

_____

_____

_____

_____

_____

_____

_____

_____

_____

_____

_____

_____

_____

### Dating Principle #3—Research and Envelopment (continued)

It's time for the good, the bad, and the ugly from the people who know you best—you, your friends and family, ex-partners, and your target great guy. What would they say are your dating strengths and opportunities:

Your perspective: _____

_____

_____

_____

_____

Your friends' and family's perspective: _____

_____

_____

_____

_____

Your ex-partners' perspective: _____

_____

_____

_____

_____

Your target guy's perspective: _____

_____

_____

_____

_____

### Dating Principle #3—Research and Envelopment (continued)

Now review the dating strengths and development areas to find the themes. Look for things that came up more than once. If your mother said it and your best friend Katie said it, then it's probably true. If your ex-boyfriend is the only one who identified a particular dating opportunity, then it's up to you to decide on the validity of his opinion. Identify your strength and opportunity themes here by filling in this chart:

| Person Giving Feedback | Great Qualities | Improvement Areas |
|---|---|---|
| Your Thoughts | | |
| Friends & Family | | |
| Ex-Partners | | |
| Target Person | | |

### *Dating Principle #3—Research and Envelopment (continued)*

From the competitive analysis and best practices discussion, hopefully you've identified five things you could tweak about your dating approach. Here's your chance to put pen to paper and commit to these tweaks.

Dating Tweak #1 _____

_____

Dating Tweak #2 _____

_____

Dating Tweak #3 _____

_____

Dating Tweak #4 _____

_____

Dating Tweak #5 _____

## Dating Principle #4—Spark-It Plan

Your personal brand describes the very best person you plan to be out on the dating scene. Go ahead and put together the goals, strengths, opportunities, and tweaks from earlier chapters. In the space provided, describe who you'll be and how you'll be perceived on the singles scene:

_____

_____

_____

_____

## Dating Principle #5— Recruitment and Affection

Just thinking about how your closest friends met their significant other is a great way to get started on finding your own great guy. So make that list right now, and you'll be off to the races:

Friend #1 is _____ and here's how she met her guy:

_____

Friend #2 is _____ and here's how she met her guy:

_____

Friend #3 is _____ and here's how she met her guy:

_____

Friend #4 is _____ and here's how she met her guy:

_____

Friend #5 is _____ and here's how she met her guy:

_____

## Dating Principle #5—Recruitment and Affection (continued)

How your friends met is a great starting point. But it's more important that you commit to five dating strategies of your own. So list them and devote that action-oriented workplace mindset to making it happen:

**1.** New Dating Recruitment Step #1 is _____

_____

**2.** New Dating Recruitment Step #2 is _____

_____

**3.** New Dating Recruitment Step #3 is _____

_____

**4.** New Dating Recruitment Step #4 is _____

_____

**5.** New Dating Recruitment Step #5 is _____

_____

# Dating Principle #6—Manage-Men

As you get a pipeline of great guys coming into your life, you want to be sure to recognize the great behaviors that are making you like them more and more. So put these ideas to paper by thinking about the guys in your dating life right now. What are they doing in an above average way that deserves a pat on the back or, at the very least, another date with you?

Guy #1 deserves recognition for _____

_____

Guy #2 deserves recognition for _____

_____

Guy #3 deserves recognition for _____

_____


## Dating Principle #6—Manage-Men (continued)

Okay, so it won't all be rosy in those early stages. We just covered the good behaviors that deserve some recognition. Now write down the things these same guys are doing that really could use some changing.

Guy #1 needs coaching and feedback on _____

_____

Guy #1 needs coaching and feedback on _____

_____

Guy #1 needs coaching and feedback on _____

_____


# Dating Principle #7—Lust-omer Service

Just as companies strive to keep their best customers onboard and their best employees at work, single women can apply a retention strategy to keep a great guy interested in staying with you. Here's your chance to write three specific retention strategies for your relationship:

Retention Strategy #1 _____

_____

Retention Strategy #2 _____

_____

Retention Strategy #3 _____

_____

## Dating Principle #8—Talent Assess-Men

One of the easiest ways to determine if you're with the right guy or wrong guy is to compare his actual personality to the guy you described in your Wishin' Statement. In the space provided, give a one-paragraph description of your current man. Consider all the same qualities you mentioned in your Wishin' Statement. The difference here is that while your Wishin' Statement had to do with aspirations, this description is your reality. It's what your guy is really like. Let's see what you come up with:

_____

_____

_____

_____

_____

_____

_____

_____

_____

### *Dating Principle #8—Talent Assess-Men (continued)*

Now that you've written a Wishin' Statement and a statement about your current guy, it's time to compare the two write-ups. Here's a scale that runs from 0 to 100 percent. On this scale, 0 means your current guy sounds absolutely nothing like your Wishin' Statement. On the flip side, 100 means your current guy sounds exactly like your Wishin' Statement. Put a mark on the scale to indicate how close your guy sounds to the one described in your Wishin' Statement:

0%---------------------------50%-------------------------100%

## Dating Principle #9—Joint Adventure

A relationship philosophy is all about achieving your joint dreams as a couple. It starts with individually deciding what you and your main squeeze want in key life categories, such as health, finances, love, career, etc. Here's a template you can use to write your solo vision for health in five key life stages. Mr. Right should do the same on a separate piece of paper. Then you'll repeat this process for each of the life categories you've agreed to discuss as a couple.

In one year, here's my vision for our approach to having and raising children:

_____

_____

In five years, here's my vision for our approach to having and raising children:

_____

_____

In ten years, here's my vision for our approach to having and raising children:

_____

_____

In twenty-five years, here's my vision for our approach to having and raising children:

_____

_____

In fifty years, here's my vision for our approach to having and raising children:

_____

_____

### Dating Principle #9—Joint Adventure (continued)

Once you have your independent visions, it's time to merge them into a unified game plan. Again, using the having and raising kids example, here's a template you can fill out together. First you need to read each other's write-ups, discuss them together as long as needed, and come to agreement on your joint plan.

Our joint vision of where we'll be in one year in regard to having and raising children:

_____

_____

Our joint vision of where we'll be in five years in regard to having and raising children:

_____

_____

Our joint vision of where we'll be in ten years in regard to having and raising children:

_____

_____

Our joint vision of where we'll be in twenty-five years in regard to having and raising children:

_____

_____

Our joint vision of where we'll be in fifty years in regard to having and raising children:

_____

_____

### Dating Principle #9—Joint Adventure (continued)

Now's the time to take action! You've arrived at the same shared vision. It's important now to break that vision down into the action steps you'll take to make it happen. Here's a template you can use to fill in your shared goals, the associated actions, due dates, and accountability for getting them done.

| Relationship Philosophy Action Plan | | | |
|---|---|---|---|
| **Life Category:** | **Visions:**<br>• Vision #1 is:_____<br>_____<br>• Vision #2 is:_____<br>_____<br>• Vision #3 is:_____<br>_____ | | |
| | **Actions:**<br>Action #1 is: _____<br>_____<br>Action #2 is: _____<br>_____<br>Action #3 is: _____<br>_____<br>Action #4 is: _____<br>_____ | **Due Date** | **Accountability** |

If you remember nothing else from this book, remember Jeff's Defs! These are the nine dating principles applied from business concepts that can dramatically improve your dating results. Here's an executive summary of Jeff's Defs, brought to you by *Dating, Inc.*

1. **Wishin' Statement** refers to what a single woman wants to find on the dating scene, what she's looking for in a guy, or what she hopes to accomplish in a future relationship.

2. **Souls are statements** outlining the long-term results, accomplishments or objectives a single woman seeks to attain in her relationships. Objectives are a specification of what is to be accomplished, the timeframe in which it is to be accomplished, and by whom.

3. **Research and Envelopment** is the process of discovering new dating and relationship knowledge and then applying that knowledge to create new and improved dating tactics.

4. **A Spark-It Plan** is a written document that details the actions necessary for a woman to achieve a specified dating objective(s).

5. **Recruitment and Affection** refers to the practice of actively seeking men to fill recently vacated or newly created relationship openings using a variety of methods.

6. **Manage-Men** is the process of maintaining or improving relationship performance by your guy through the use of dating

assessment tools, coaching, and counseling, as well as providing continuous (okay, how about intermittent) feedback.

7. **Lust-omer Service** is the set of behaviors that a savvy, successful woman undertakes during her interactions with a great guy.

8. **Talent Assess-Men** refers to the process of measuring a man's current dating performance versus future dating potential to determine the long-term value of the man to your relationship.

9. **Joint Adventure** is a strategic alliance between two people to undertake a life together.

# appendix three
# business terms applied to dating

Throughout this book, you heard about our SuperStar Network of savvy business-women and -men. One of the questions we asked each of them was to describe a business phrase, term, or concept that they believed could be applied to dating and relationships. Here's a compilation of some of the best business terms from our SuperStar Network and how each one works in the world of dating and relationships.

### Application process

If you break up with a boyfriend and are now back on the market, it's time to initiate an application process. This is where you announce to the world of eligible men that you're free and are now accepting applications to the open position of "my boyfriend"!—Caroline, restaurant manager, Wichita, Kansas

### Candidate evaluation and review

Finding your significant other or developing your primary relationship can be considered the most important "hire" that you make. One should have a very refined sense of the criteria they're looking for and be careful to soberly and objectively evaluate whether or not the "candidate" can meet your needs. Once in the relationship, you should constantly evaluate whether or not the person (and the relationship) is working out. You have to keep evaluating until you get to the point where you have absolute trust in the relationship and partner involved.—Mannie, small business owner, Sioux City, Iowa

### Downsizing and right sizing

It's important to eliminate the unproductive parts of a relationship. These include the behaviors and practices that sabotage relationships. The key is to refocus energies around core strengths and goals, especially if either person feels overextended.—Ricky, business consultant, Santa Fe, New Mexico

### Integrated approach

In social work, an integrated approach means drawing on a person's strengths to improve their situation and involving as many positive people in their community to support them as possible. This could easily be applied to the dating world. If you draw on your strengths and tap into all your resources, you improve your chances of success. For instance, if you have a friend who has tons of friends, ask that person to put the word out for you and have him/her be your agent for dating.—Catharine, magazine editor, London, England

### Quality assurance

During the life of the project, our clients will often hire a third party for quality assurance. They will attend all of our meetings and read all of our deliverables. Their goal is to basically make sure we're not taking advantage of our client. They are sort of like the role of a relative or close friend in relationships. They ask a lot of questions to make sure the person you're dating isn't taking advantage of you.—Rhonda, fashion designer, Providence, Rhode Island

### Total compensation

You have to understand and communicate all the positive things a person brings to a relationship, especially the less obvious ones. For example, in a business setting, employees often think of compensation as only salary and retirement contributions, even though they are receiving other value as well (for instance, employer subsidy for health care coverage, stock options).—Dolly, architect, Hilton Head, South Carolina

## Attraction, development, and retention

To be successful in ensuring the right talent is in the right job at the right time, you need to work at all three dimensions. This applies to the dating world as "right person, right relationship, right time." Most people really don't spend the time identifying what they want from the relationship. We think we know what we want or what we are able to compromise on until we are tested and realize we don't want to compromise on certain things. We need to learn to formulate and ask the "right" questions early in the dating relationship that will give us true insights to see if the individual is compatible to your beliefs, values, and desires in life.—Cecilia, chef, Detroit, Michigan

### Performance reviews

I believe performance reviews help minimize surprises for performance expectations in any type of organization. Performance reviews can be applied in a relationship or dating situation—I would even call it something like shared goals and aspirations for dating. This way the couple knows what to expect of each other during the relationship and could avoid some misdirected conversations or actions. A single person could also benefit from outlining their goals and expectations (and eventually performance reviews) so that as they began dating or using dating services, they were pretty clear about themselves. This should only serve to help them as they "assess potential dating candidates."—Scottie, healthcare consultant, Portland, Oregon

### Work plan

A work plan is an approach teams or departments might take to get a particular task done or a project launched. I have a friend who decided to make a "Catch a Husband" plan. She had success metrics and target measures on the number of dates per week. She placed herself on an online dating site, asked all her friends to start to set her up, etc. Sometimes she even made brunch, lunch, afternoon drink, and dinner plans in one day. She even gave them "feedback" if she didn't think it could work out.—Tanisha, TV anchor, Chicago, Illinois

### Finding the right job fit

Most applicants and hiring managers spend lots of time matching technical competencies for a position but typically do not spend enough time on job fit—matching values, culture, and work style. These are extremely important for a successful match between employer and employee as with dating and relationships. As an experienced leader in a major corporation, I have seen many technically talented people not able to succeed in a company due to differences in culture and values. If more time was spent assessing this prior to employment, you would have a better chance of choosing the best person for the job. With dating, the same could be said for successful relationships.—Colleen, retail shop owner, Melbourne, Australia

### Self-assessment

My dating life has been colorful. I have dated many men over the past fifteen years and have had numerous relationships. My friends gave me the nickname "Eight-monther" because a majority of my relationships concluded in month eight. Not month seven or month nine, month eight. Upon reflecting on my love life, or doing a love life "self-assessment," I've noticed that most of my relationships began and ended the same way. A man shows interest and pursues the relationship . . . the honeymoon phase is blissful . . . at month seven I begin asking hard-hitting questions . . . then I realize I've selected a man that is in no way appropriate for me. He's either too young, too neurotic, or too flaky. I try to ignore it and by month eight, I realize I'm living a lie and as much as it pains me to do it, I break up with him.—Wilma, limo driver, Hartford, Connecticut

### Cost benefit analysis

In business, you need to determine the costs and benefits of various alternatives to make a sound decision. The same is true as you consider personal relationships. At times, we may become aware of our partner's shortcomings. This could create some tension and force someone to question their relationship and whether or not to continue. This is where I believe a cost benefit analysis can be helpful. It may sound crude, but weighing the positive qualities of your partner and the benefits of a close, loving relationship (support, love, companionship, good cook, humor, laughter, back rubs, etc.) against the alternatives can help in accepting some of the shortcomings and realizing the great benefits of your relationship. I also think it keeps us "consciously" in love and actively involved in our relationships. Finally, I think going through this analysis can help to remind us of the very reasons we fell in love with our partner in the first place and keep the love and passion alive.—Liza, receptionist, Dover, Delaware

## Joint venture

Relationships are like trying to structure and run a joint venture. At first when you are looking for partners, you sort of go after the best-looking one, hoping that when you peek under the hood, there are the same interests, beliefs, approach to business, and hopefully some financial means to get the joint venture on its feet. Meeting the partner for the first time is tentative; you are nervous and not sure how they will react to your suggestions. In your first full meeting, you are trying to sell yourself a bit as well as dig for information that will help you evaluate whether or not the partner can satisfy your needs. Of course, some companies jump right into the sack and try to launch something too quickly and find out pretty fast that the other company is too needy or just doesn't have the equipment to get the job done. However, in most joint ventures that get off the ground, the parties agree to share the efforts and spoils fifty-fifty. Michelle, freelance copywriter, Salt Lake City, Utah

## Expectations management

I believe this is more important than anything as it is done poorly in relationships as well as business. Issues mostly occur when the outcome of a situation is different than what an individual expected. For some reason, even when people know a situation will produce a negative result, they would rather try to deal with it afterwards than discuss it openly beforehand. It may be tough, but it builds trust and above all manages expectations.—Bradley, investment banker, New York

## Orientation

In business, orientation represents the activities or plans used to help acclimate people into a new company or a new job. It often includes sharing the corporate vision, mission, who's who, roles and responsibilities, etc. Sometimes a ninety-day learning plan is developed with activities and actions to help bring the new hire up to speed. In the dating world, orientation represents activities or discussions used to help your new boyfriend or girlfriend get acclimated to dating you. This often includes discussing your expectations about the relationship (not looking for anything serious right now, just want to have fun, looking for the right one, etc.), roles and responsibilities/rules as it pertains to dating (call when you say you are going to call, be on time for dates, rules on canceling a date, etc.), aligning your interests and life goals (hobbies, family, job/career interests, education, etc.).—Randal, restaurant owner, Cleveland, Ohio

### Market Analysis

You could perform a market analysis in dating to observe and note a prospect's behavior so that you can better predict their responses to certain situations and proposals. It's a buyer's market when there are plenty of great prospects available to choose from. It becomes a seller's market when a lot of people are competing for the same single person's attention.—Stefanie, environmentalist, London, England

### Change management

Change management is effective at work because we understand that change is more difficult for some people than it is for others, we don't expect everyone to embrace the change or be at the same place in the change management curve, and we consciously and thought-fully plan and provide tools to encourage change. There are two main change management principles that can be applied to dating. First, you have to understand that you and your partner may not always be in sync, but you can be aware of that and work through those times that you are not in sync. Second, during change, we encourage frequent communications, and we suggest that it's better to overcommunicate than undercommunicate. The same is true for relationships—espe-cially new relationships.—Stephen, software programmer, Pittsburgh, Pennsylvania

### *You Got Something to Say?*

Our SuperStar Network is always growing. If you have a business term that you believe applies to dating, email it to *contact@datinginc book.com*. Who knows, you just might end up listed on our Web site or in a future book. So let's hear what you have to say!

# appendix four
# start your own SuperStar network book club

Are you looking to form your own SuperStar Network? There's nothing like some new friends to grow your social circle or stimulate great conversation with your current friends or colleagues. Plus, you just might meet someone who can set you up. At your first meeting, be sure to assign everyone *Dating, Inc.* to read. Why? Well, it will help get the word out for Carol and me that proven business tactics can be applied to dating and relationships. Plus, you'll immediately have something in common to talk about at your first get-together.

Now, it's entirely possible that everyone will read *Dating, Inc.*, come to your first book club meeting, and look at you intently, waiting for you to kick off the meeting. We don't want you sweating your new SuperStar Network leadership role, so here are some questions you can raise for some juicy, thought-provoking discussion together:

1. Describe a business phrase, term, or concept that you believe can be applied to dating and relationships. How does it apply? For example, recruitment and selection plans are used by companies to find an ideal candidate for a job. In the dating world, a Recruitment and Affection plan could be used to find the ideal person for a relationship. So get creative and be descriptive—anything goes here. Plus, don't forget to submit your dating business terms to *contact@datingincbook.com*. We can't wait to hear all your great ideas.

2. Why do you believe that some single women are really successful at work but have trouble finding a great guy?

3. What are some of the must-have, nice-to-have, and who-cares qualities that you look for when meeting new guys?

4. What are some of the most important do's and don'ts for your first day on the job? How about do's and don'ts for first dates?

5. How did your five closest attached friends and family members meet? What are some more places you could add to the list of great ways to meet someone new?

6. What does it take to lead a successful negotiation at work? Can you see parallels in reaching compromises in a relationship?

7. What role does reward and recognition play at work? Would there be a way to incorporate reward and recognition into keeping a great guy interested?

8. What should a couple do if one partner is really adventurous between the sheets, but the other partner is more conservative?

9. Couples spend months planning every last detail of their wedding but often little time planning the rest of their lives together. What topics do you believe a couple should discuss to build a quality life together?

## Start Your Own SuperStar Network Book Club: Part 2

Just because we like to think in nines, it doesn't mean we can't provide a second list of nine. So if your SuperStar Network Book Club breezes through the first nine questions, here are nine bonus questions to really get the conversation going.

1. What is the absolute best and worst advice you can think of when it comes to being successful in relationships?

2. Do you believe there are any strategies you've followed at work to be successful that you've been able to apply (or could see applying) in your relationships to be happy?

3. What are some of the best ice-breakers you've ever seen at a work function or meeting? How could some of these be applied to ease the tension on a first date?

4. What makes change management effective at work? How could these principles be applied to dating?

5. What approach do you take in providing coaching and feedback to an employee or colleague? Could any of these principles work in dealing with relationship challenges?

6. What are the most common reasons a company builds loyalty with their customers? Why do companies sometimes lose loyal customers? Are there things a single woman could do to build loyalty with her man?

7. What role do you believe performance reviews play in an organization? Why don't people dating or in relationships ever check in on their performance? How would this work if a single person wanted to do a performance review on themselves or the person they're dating?

8. What is the worst mistake you ever made in a relationship? What would you do differently if you had another chance?

9. What are the most important aspects for a business relationship to survive over time? Are there similar or different qualities that are critical to a romantic relationship surviving in the long run?

# appendix five
# an interview with carol and jeff cohen

Do you ever get asked the same question so many times you wish you could just publish a list of frequently asked questions (FAQs) to once and for all provide the answers? We know exactly how you feel! That's why we've compiled the nine most popular questions right here in a nice and tidy list. Why nine questions? Well, we met on the ninth of January and got married on the ninth of November, so the number nine holds a special place in our heart.

If you're one of our loyal readers, this is your chance to get to know the authors better.

**Question #1:** Business can be approached logically, but dating and relationships are matters of the heart. Can you really apply logical skills to an emotional subject?

Emotions versus logic can get tricky. We agree that it's much easier to approach work from a logical place. When you turn to dating and relationships, all the emotions do creep in. However, by applying business concepts to romance, we're not advocating getting rid of emotions entirely. The idea is to approach finding the right person from a logical place. Once you find him, by all means let the emotions flood back in and decide from your heart if he's really right for you in the long run. But if you're letting emotions completely guide your approach to dating, it can paralyze your thinking.

**Question #2:** Where did the idea come from to apply business principles to dating and relationships?

Working in a corporation, Jeff started to develop a reputation for getting things done. He was Mr. Execution, someone who could be counted on to deliver. Day after day he'd get e-mails from his boss asking him to make something so. No matter the request, initiative, project, or task, he could visualize the desired end goal, break it down into action steps, and execute on the plan to make it happen. Despite his success at work, something was missing in his personal life. He really wanted to find a wife. Unfortunately, he didn't even have a girlfriend at the time. After many emotional days and months complaining to his friends and family, it hit him. He was using all these business principles successfully at work. Why not apply them to finding a wife? That was the precise moment he visualized an e-mail from his boss asking him to find a spouse. For the first time, he thought about dating in business terms. Light bulbs were flashing in his head telling him he was on to something big. This was about to change his entire outlook on dating and single life forever.

**Question #3:** Is it really true Jeff went on 77 blind dates before he met Carol?

This is absolutely true! If you don't believe Jeff, he'd be happy to provide the names and phone numbers from his little black book. Oh, wait a minute, Carol made him burn the little black book on their wedding night. Seriously, by thinking from a business perspective, Jeff designed a methodical dating program to attract more women and find the best possible one of his dreams. Complete with goals and objectives, an action plan and timeline, his dating program consisted of things like three trips to singles-themed Club Med resorts, one gold membership in a dating service, four Hamptons summer shares and one Jersey Shore house, 300 nights in Manhattan and New Jersey pubs ogling, flirting, and in some cases leaving with phone numbers scribbled on napkins and coasters, and seventy-seven blind dates. On blind date number seventy-eight, he met Carol, now his wife and coauthor.

**Question #4:** Do you believe that successful, savvy business-women need to find a man to be happy?

It's not our place to tell anyone what they need in their life to be truly happy. What we do know is that we've seen so many successful women rise straight up through the glass ceiling, start new businesses, and reach their career potential. At the same time, we've watched many of these women sacrifice in their personal lives to keep their careers on track. We believe every woman deserves the best of both worlds, and that's the mission of *Dating, Inc.* We want to teach women how to apply business principles they already know or can easily learn to meet more great guys and find the right one for them. That does not mean women have to find a man to be fulfilled. But if it's something that's important to them, then *Dating, Inc.* is honored to provide a roadmap to success!

**Question #5:** Do you have to be a successful businesswoman looking for a man to benefit from the material covered in *Dating, Inc.?*

Let's get one thing straight right away. This book is not just for currently super-successful single businesswomen! If you ever held a job, any job at all, at some point in your career, you'll relate to the concepts in this book. More simply, if you've ever held a job, then you can find a man. From corporate vice presidents to restaurant waitresses, we're all familiar with customers, sales, hiring and firing, and bosses. This book will show you how these concepts you already use in your everyday life will help you recruit, select, and retain the right man for a relationship. Also, don't think you have to fall under the "never been married" heading to benefit from this book. If you're single, separated, divorced, widowed, straight or gay, keep reading! As long as you're looking for a partner, this book is for you.

**Question #6:** What if you're a guy, can you still benefit from *Dating, Inc.*?

Absolutely! Anyone who no longer wants to depend on fate to find their mate can benefit from *Dating, Inc.* Remember, Jeff's a guy (or so his driver's license claims) and he put himself through this dating plan to find Carol. So by all means guys, take your left hand off the remote control, take your right hand off that pint of beer, pick up a copy of *Dating, Inc.*, and polish up your dating skills. After the women finish reading this book, you're going to need every advantage you can get just to land a date with them.

**Question #7:** What exactly is a SuperStar Network and how did they help in writing *Dating, Inc.*?

As the About.com Guide to Dating and Relationships, Jeff is a dating expert, and living proof that a dating plan really works. As a successful businesswoman who has also been successful in relationships (at least Jeff would like to believe Carol thinks she's been successful in relationships), Carol can represent the women. Carol and Jeff together have a lot to say, but real-life examples from single and married women and men add valuable insights, inspiration, and examples that illustrate the concepts in the book. So we relied on a business principle, networking, to gather stories, advice, and anecdotes from our SuperStar Network. These are people we grew up with, went to school with, worked with, met at the gym, sat next to on planes, or just chatted up for no particular reason. They're a truly worldwide network residing in various places across the globe including the United States, Europe, Asia, and Australia. We tried to make a friend in Antarctica, but the penguins had no comment.

**Question #8:** What exactly is a relationship philosophy, and why should all couples have one?

We already know couples spend months planning every last detail of their wedding together. They choose the grooviest band, the prettiest flowers, the tastiest cake, the coolest reception hall, and the snazziest wedding invitations. All for an event that usually lasts four hours or less. What about the rest of their lives together? This is where a relationship philosophy comes in. It's the guiding principles for couples that want to merge their lives together with the least amount of disruption and make their relationships work. It's how couples develop a short- and long-term relationship plan and get on the road to achieving their joint dreams as a couple. To develop a successful relationship philosophy, it's important for couples to discuss and agree on key life categories like love, career, health, finances, family, home, friendships, personal development, and values.

**Question #9:** There are so many dating and relationship books in the market, what makes *Dating, Inc.* different?

We're tired of hearing about quick fixes and short cuts. *Dating, Inc.* is not a magical program that will net you a new partner in ten minutes or less, guaranteed. It is, however, a carefully constructed plan that will get results if you make the commitment and follow the steps. We've broken it down into steps so that it will not feel intimidating, overwhelming, or confusing. All you have to do is believe in the process, believe in yourself, and take the first step. Pretty soon you'll be landing more dates, meeting better-quality partners, and maybe even finding your soul mate. At the very least you'll be taking charge of your love life and not relying on fate to find your mate.

So if you've been settling for the wrong guy, latching on to just any okay guy, or avoiding the dating scene entirely, then *Dating, Inc.* is for you. This book will teach you how to apply the business skills you already know, or could easily learn, to land more dates and ultimately find your soul mate. You already know how to create success in your business life. *Dating, Inc.* will teach you how to redirect these success skills to your love life.

# index

# about the authors

## Jeff Cohen, Dating and Relationship Expert

Jeff Cohen is the About.com Guide to Dating and Relationships and a columnist for Yahoo!Personals. As a frequent media contributor, he's been interviewed by *USA Today, New York Daily News, MSN, Chicago Tribune, Boston Herald*, and the *Denver Post*, and appeared on CNN as well as a special Voice of America dating program, airing to over 100 million listeners globally. Jeff has performed standup comedy at Caroline's, The Comic Strip Live, and New York Comedy Club. Jeff received a dual degree in marketing from the Wharton School of Business and psychology from the University of Pennsylvania. He's also not afraid to admit it took seventy-seven blind dates before he found the one.

## Carol Cohen, M.B.A.

Carol Cohen has held a variety of senior level executive positions in the retail, technology, and financial services industries, including Vice President of Organizational Capabilities and Talent Development at American Express. She received her M.B.A. with a focus on international business from the University of Colorado. Carol has appeared on *Good Morning America* and was also blind date number seventy-eight for Jeff.

## Carol and Jeff

Carol and Jeff were introduced by the head of recruitment and selection at American Express. Jeff views the engagement ring as his ultimate retention strategy. Carol has had Jeff on a development plan ever since. After their merger, Carol and Jeff acquired a house, and now regularly mix business with pleasure.